INTERNET UK
in easy steps

Chris Russell

COMPUTER STEP

In easy steps is an imprint of Computer Step
Southfield Road . Southam
Warwickshire CV33 OFB . England

Tel: 01926 817999 Fax: 01926 817005
http://www.computerstep.com

Reprinted 1999
3rd edition 1998
2nd edition 1997
1st edition 1996

Notice of Liability
Every effort has been made to ensure that this book contains accurate
and current information. However, Computer Step and the author shall
not be liable for any loss or damage suffered by readers as a result of
any information contained herein.

Trademarks
All trademarks are acknowledged as belonging to their respective
companies.

Printed and bound in the United Kingdom

ISBN 1-84078-006-1

Contents

First Steps

In this chapter you'll find out how the Internet came to exist, along with an overview of what it has now become. You'll also learn about the PC hardware and software that you need to access the Internet, how to choose a suitable Internet Service Provider and even a little about the future directions the Internet is likely to take.

Chapter One

Covers

The Net: Past, Present and Future

The Internet (which we'll call the Net from now on because everyone who uses it does) started out as a US military program designed to enable research centres to keep in touch and exchange information more efficiently.

This was way back in 1969. At the time it was called Arpanet (for Advanced Research Projects Agency). To begin with it consisted of just four computers at universities in Utah, Los Angeles, Santa Barbara and Stanford.

By 1972 it consisted of 50 computers. The UK didn't really join in until the end of the seventies when the first academic network called JANET (Joint Academic Network) was established between five UK universities.

At this stage most of the computer networks in the US and Europe had few connections to other networks. Only in the 1980s did networks begin to interconnect. This was when the term Internet first came into use.

One major problem with creating the Internet was the need to use a standardised networking method. This is called TCP/IP for Transmission Control Protocol/Internet Protocol. It's a bit of a mouthful but you'll see the initials so often it's worth knowing what they mean.

and now...

The Net's really spectacular growth began in the early 1990s. The invention of the Web combined with telephone access made it easy to connect to the Net and to use it.

Growth quickly became so frantic that it's now impossible to count the number of computers on the Net – although 1997 estimates suggest there are tens of millions and that the numbers are growing at thousands per week.

This brings up an important point: no one owns the Net or is responsible for it. Individuals, companies and organisations of all kinds own parts of it but the Net itself is a co-operative effort.

HANDY TIP

The Internet is still young and many of those who were there at the beginning are still there. The old hands can be a little terse with newbies - new Net users - but don't worry if it seems strange. You'll be an old hand yourself by the time you've finished this book and practised for a few days.

This has certain consequences. For a start, there's no official body to complain to if you don't like something someone is doing on the Net.

It also means anyone with an idea can implement it on the Net. New uses are invented all the time at such a rate that people speak of Internet Time, where things change at a far higher rate than in the 'real' world.

This is possible because the Net is largely software – change the software and you change the Internet. Invent new software and you can add a new service.

Most of these new services are attempts by entrepreneurs to find ways to make money from the Net. These revolve around familiar ideas: providing entertainment and selling goods and services.

In practice, because the Net is interactive, entertainment and services tend to overlap. For example, as we'll see later, multiplayer action games are catching on fast. This isn't entertainment in the same sense as TV delivers, but then again, it isn't simply selling computer games. It's a completely new service made possible by the Net.

The great thing about all these new Net services, though, is that you can usually try them for free. Some will appeal, some won't, but there's something on the Net for everyone.

The future

You're incredibly lucky to be experiencing the Net at a time when it's changing the way we live.

You're coming to it at one of the most exciting times in its history. It's never been easier to use and it's never been more exciting to participate.

Net access will soon be universal, faster and a part of our everyday working and social life. The next generation will be as unable to imagine life without the Net as a life without the aeroplane, TV and telephone.

The Hardware you Need

This book assumes you already have or are buying a PC, though much of it applies if you have a different computer such as an Apple Mac, for example.

Basically, to connect to the Internet from home you need a PC, a telephone line and a modem.

Net users tend to find themselves online for long periods of time. While you're using the telephone line to access the Net others can't make or receive phone calls, so a second line can save a lot of family arguments.

A modem (which stands for Modulator/Demodulator) converts the digital signals used by your PC into tones suitable for a telephone line. It also converts them back again. This enables you to send and receive information to and from other computers on the Net using your ordinary telephone line. This is currently the simplest option.

The latest modems can transmit and receive data at 56,000 bits per second (56K), which is about 7,000 bytes per second. To put this into context, it would take about three minutes to send the data on a full floppy disk to someone else over the Net at this speed.

When you buy a modem look for these features:

1   V.90 (which means it's a 56K modem).

2   Fax support (you can send and receive faxes).

3   Voice support (it can act as an answering machine).

It doesn't matter whether it's an internal or external modem, they work in the same way. However, an internal modem will be slightly cheaper while an external modem is easier to install.

56K Modems

Until late 1997 it was strongly held that 33.6K was the fastest speed a modem could achieve over standard telephone lines.

Happily for Internet users enterprising engineers in America discovered that it was indeed possible to transfer data faster, at a much more impressive 56K. Using high compression rates, the theory was that data could now rocket across the world's telephone lines, making those with the necessary computer equipment much more productive in their Net use.

The reality of the theory fell a little short and for various (highly) technical reasons the modern 56K modem will receive data at anything to up 56K but can send it at only 33.6K.

While this may sound a little limiting it isn't as the majority of modem users download and receive a lot more information than they send.

Today, nearly all ISPs support 56K modems through a technical standard known as V90. V90 arose from a long-running battle between modem experts US Robotics and Rockwell Communications which each created their own high speed modem technologies. US Robotics called theirs X2 whilst Rockwell plumped for 56k Flex.

In an effort to unify the transfer protocols and make life easier for the consumer, both sides were persuaded to get together and agree the standard so if you hear the phrases X2 and 56K Flex do not be alarmed! Many modems which adhered to one or the other of the standards were pre-equipped with special hardware which can be updated through software to be fully V90 compliant.

Internet Service Providers

An Internet Service Provider, or ISP is also known as an Internet Access Provider, or IAP. The terms are interchangeable.

An ISP has computers, called servers, which remain permanently connected to other computers on the Net via high speed data links.

BEWARE

Most new PCs come with a modem and a trial connection to one or more ISPs. However, you don't have to use the one supplied with your PC. Any ISP can provide you with a Net connection.

Each ISP is a small (or sometimes large) part of the Internet and owns its computers. It usually leases links to other computers on the Internet from cable and telephone companies who specialise in data transmission.

The ISP also owns a lot of modems built into large racks which connect to the telephone system. You normally connect to the ISP via a modem and your telephone line.

Your call to the your ISP is normally charged at local call rates. This money goes to BT, Mercury or your cable company. Your ISP normally charges a flat monthly fee regardless of how long you use the Net.

Some ISPs only offer a local service, but most now offer national coverage at local call rates. Some are even beginning to offer a global service, providing low cost access to the Net via your ISP from anywhere in the world.

Choosing an ISP

Competition among ISPs is intense, and these days there's little to choose between them. However, here's a check list of questions to ask before signing up, and the kind of answers you should expect to get:

1   Do you have local call access throughout the UK? (Yes)

2   Is your telephone support desk open seven days a week? (Yes)

3   Are there sign-up or other extra charges? (No)

4   Do you supply self installing Net software? (Yes)

5   Do you supply an Internet software suite? (Yes)

6   What's your modem ratio? (10:1 is good, 20:1 is bad)

7   Do you support 56K? (Yes, but is it X2, K56Flex or V90)

8   Do you support POP3 e-mail access? (Yes)

9   Can you have multiple e-mail accounts? (Yes)

10   Do you provide free Web space? (Yes, 5MB or more)

11   Are FrontPage server extensions supported? (Yes)

12   Can you use CGI scripts on your Web pages? (Yes)

13   How much unscheduled downtime have you had? (None)

14   Can I cancel the contract at any time? (Yes)

 REMEMBER

Never stay with an ISP if you're not happy with it. Most offer free trials so it usually costs nothing to check them out.

The Software you Need

In principle, each service on the Net requires its own special software called a client. However, all of the basic popular services are supported in the two leading Web browsers. At the time of writing, these are Netscape Communicator and Microsoft Internet Explorer.

For PC users running Windows there's no argument over which is easiest to use – Internet Explorer (abbreviated to IE4 for version 4 or IE5 for version 5), is the best. It's free too, so we'll use it to illustrate net services and how to get the most out of them.

Internet Explorer is seamlessly integrated into Windows 98, so you don't need to download it.

It's available direct from Microsoft's Web site at:

`http://www.microsoft.com/ie`

Or you can get it on CD-ROM by phoning Microsoft Customer Support on 0345 002000.

For problem-free Net use, run the right type of software. If you're using Windows 95/98 then you should only run 32-bit Net software designed for it. Under Windows 3.1 you should run 16-bit Windows software.

All ISPs also provide Net access software suites when you sign up with them or accept their free trial offers. These may use other software, but will do the same basic jobs as Internet Explorer and access the same Net services.

In fact there are hundreds of free, shareware and commercial Net software products available to access Net services, many of which offer more features than the components of Internet Explorer or Netscape Communicator. These can all be obtained from the Net itself as we'll see a little later on in chapters three and ten.

Microsoft Internet Explorer has everything you need to get started – and it's free!

...cont'd

There's no need to try to master all of the services on the Net at once. As you become more confident you can try them out and continue with those that appeal to you.

Specialist Net services

While Internet Explorer or Netscape Communicator can handle all of the most common Net service requirements there are also specialist services you will be interested in trying. These require separate software.

1. IRC

Internet Relay Chat is actually quite an old service by Net standards. Basically, it enables you to hold text based conversations with any number of other people. It's extremely popular with teenagers.

2. Net telephony

Unlike IRC, Net telephony is intended to enable person-to-person or private conferencing. It supports audio, video, application sharing, file exchange, whiteboarding (where you and others can all share the same whiteboard online) and other features such as enabling one person to take others on a tour of the Web.

3. 3D worlds

One of the holy grails of the Net is to provide online worlds where people can meet using representations of themselves called avatars. Some are extremely strange.

4. On-line games

Many of the most successful PC games such as Quake can be played with others on a network, including the Net. But some companies, such as TEN and Kali, are now offering more sophisticated persistent gaming worlds that you can visit at any time and simply join in.

One of the fastest areas of growth on the Net is online gaming environments. Quake showed the way.

The ISDN Alternative

Both the Net and your PC are based on digital technology, which basically means all data is sent as strings of ones and zeros. Interestingly, the PSTN (Public Switched Telephone System) is also digital, apart from the small section joining your home/office to the local exchange. This short section is called the Local Loop, and uses analogue technology. This is ideal for carrying voice but terrible for data transmission.

One solution is ISDN, Integrated Services Digital Network. This converts your local loop to digital technology. It's faster than a modem and offers other advantages.

Consumer ISDN is properly called ISDN-2. What this provides is two 64Kbit connections called bearer or B channels and a 16Kbit data channel, which confusingly isn't used for data. BT use it to set up the call.

The two 64Kbit B channels each have their own number and you can use them as two separate voice or data lines. They can also be aggregated to form a single 128Kbit link.

64Kbit gives you a basic data transmission speed of 6.4K per second. With data compression it often seems a lot faster.

A call made on an ISDN line has a second major advantage: it only takes 0.7 seconds, on average, to set up a call compared with around 30 seconds using a standard analogue connection.

Converting to ISDN currently costs more for line rental than analogue calls but the actual cost of calls is exactly the same. This may change as it's actually in BT's interests for you to use ISDN.

If you use the Net enough to justify a second telephone line consider going over to ISDN instead. Contact BT on 150 in the first instance or visit its Web site at:

http://www.bt.com

Coming Soon

As the Web becomes more of a multimedia environment used to carry still images, moving video, animations, programs and even voice calls, the speed limitations on the local loop become ever more onerous.

This is known as the bandwidth problem. Bandwidth is the term used to describe the data carrying capacity of a particular data transmission system. It's always limited to the speed of the slowest section of the link – in this case, the section between your home/office and the exchange.

There are, though, a number of high bandwidth data delivery technologies waiting eagerly in the wings which can be used to improve the situation.

Cable modems

If you have cable coming into your home you probably already know your cable company can offer cheaper phone calls. However, in theory the cable can be used to carry a massive amount of digital data.

Cable companies are rushing to convert their systems to enable two way data transmission and will be offering cable modem connections to the Net at speeds of up to 10MBits per second. This is 1.25MB per second (200,000 times) faster than ISDN.

Cable modems provide a permanent, full time connection but each 10Mbit link is shared between up to 2,000 people.

Radio modems

The UK Government has already sold licences to several companies who plan to deliver the Net to you over what's called a fixed radio link.

This works in a similar way to a mobile phone but because the aerials are fixed (among other more technical reasons) a great deal more data can be sent in a given time.

Radio links will probably take longer to arrive than cable modems and will be available first to businesses.

Powering-up data delivery

In October 1997, UK power and communications companies NorWeb and Nortel announced a new technology capable of delivering up to 1MB per second of data from the Internet to the home using the cables carrying your electricity supply.

The Net's constantly increasing demands on bandwidth mean we're likely to see other methods of delivering it before long. Even satellite delivery is a possibility for the next millennium.

As with the cable modems a number of users will have to share the 1MB channel, but on the plus side the new technology should be remarkably cheap.

It has one other major advantage for home users which will change the way we use the Net: with the Norweb solution you will be permanently connected to the Net. You won't have to dial in to a service provider.

This means, for example, that with the right software on your PC you can access not just the Net but your own home PC, and anything it's connected to (your video recorder for example), at any time from anywhere in the world.

Digital Subscriber Line

Waiting in the wings is DSL, a clever technique which enables at least 8MBits per second to be downloaded to you over the local telephone loop (with about 1.8MBit uploads).

This works well, is relatively cheap and is already being used by some US companies. Moreover, you get the whole of the available bandwidth for your own use.

However, in the UK implementing DSL requires the cooperation of BT, which owns the local loop, and BT doesn't want to do it because it will mean it does more work for less money.

However, the threat of cable modems and Net data delivery over the domestic power cables will probably force BT into what passes for action where it's concerned.

Let's all hope DSL fares better than ISDN, which was originally made available in 1980 and is only now being heavily promoted by BT as a consumer service.

Getting Connected

When you access the Internet you're actually joining a real computer network just like those used within companies. To do this you need networking software. Windows 95/98 comes with the required software but it has to be set up.

Some ISPs provide installation software capable of doing this setting up for you. In this chapter you'll learn how to set up the Windows networking software for yourself in order to gain a better understanding of the issues.

Covers

Chapter Two

Windows Networking Overview

Windows 95 (and Windows 98) is heavily oriented toward networking, which includes the Net. And compared with just a few years ago it's now relatively easy for even new users to set it up.

There are basically three areas you need to address: installing Dial-Up Networking software, installing networking software and setting up the networking software.

Dial-Up Networking is the top level software you use to specify the ISP you're connecting to and to initiate the connection from your PC. Basically, it's the bit you click.

Because the Net is a real network you need network drivers to access it. The Windows Net software comes in several parts: a client, an adaptor and a protocol. Each of which has to be added to Windows.

Once the necessary networking software has been installed it has to be configured. This is the final step. Once this is done correctly you can establish a connection with the Net and use your Net software; browsers, e-mail applications and so on over the link.

In this chapter you'll find out how to install and configure all of the required networking software supplied with Windows for Net access. Follow it through in order and you should have no problems.

 There are a number of sources of further information on setting up Windows 95/98 Net access. For example, see Networking in easy steps, or Networking with Windows 98 in easy steps, in this same series.

Installing Dial-Up Networking

Check to see if Dial-Up Networking is already installed on your PC. Double click on My Computer. If there is a folder inside it labelled Dial-Up Networking double click on it. Inside should be an icon labelled Make New Connection.

If you don't see it, open Control Panel from the Start menu and select Add/Remove Programs. Click on the Windows Setup tab and select Communications. Click on Details and see if the checkbox next to Dial-Up Networking has a tick in it. If not, put one in and click on OK. You will now be asked for your Windows CD-ROM to install it.

When adding new components using Windows setup don't untick anything already installed or it will be removed.

1 From Control Panel click on Add/Remove Programs and then select the Windows Setup tab.

2 Click on the Communications entry and Details. Select Dial-Up Networking.

3 You should now be able to see a new folder in My Computer.

Installing Network Drivers

From Control Panel, double-click on the Network icon. There will normally be nothing at all in the Configuration window, so it's time to add the parts you need. Click on the Add button.

This brings up a dialogue box called Select Network Component Type. Select Client and yet another dialogue box appears with various options. You want the Microsoft client.

This process is repeated from the Select Network Component Type dialogue box as shown below in order to install the Adapter and Protocol networking components.

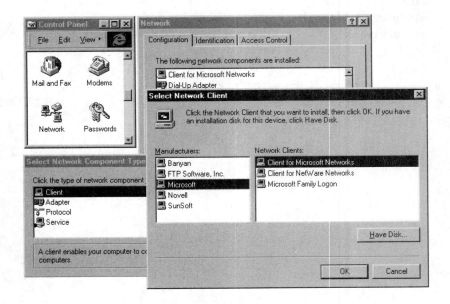

The networking components necessary to enable you to access the Internet using Dial-Up Networking are installed from the Network icon in Control Panel.

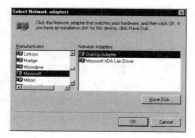

2 From the Network Adapter list choose Microsoft and Dial-Up Adapter. This is software that pretends to be a PC network card.

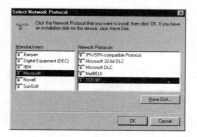

3 From the Protocol list choose Microsoft and then TCP/IP.

HANDY TIP

If you get confused or add the wrong component simply select it from the Network dialogue box and click on the Remove button, then Add the correct component.

4 The Network dialogue box should now look like this. Older versions of Windows 95 won't show the arrow and text following TCP/IP.

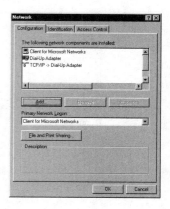

At this stage you've installed the components to enable you to access the Net, but they haven't yet been configured for your particular ISP. This is the next step. However, it won't necessarily be exactly the same procedure for each ISP, so we're going to step through the most common set up sequence and discuss alternative configuration requirements in the main text.

The Information you Need

The amount of information you need to configure Dial-Up Networking and the Windows network drivers varies. It depends on how your ISP has set up its service. Because the various items often seem to make no more sense than the incantations used by magicians, we've listed the various items of information you may be given, provided an example and explained why you need them.

Local Access Number – eg: 0345 336576
The local call rate number you dial to reach your ISP's modems. You may get several of these with a preferred order of use.

ID – eg: compstep
Your name on the service. This may be allocated to you or you may be able to specify a name. If you're given one you can often define an alias for it once you're actually on the service.

Password – eg: kori4prez
Used to prove your identity. Your first one will be allocated by the ISP. If you can change it then do so regularly and never divulge it to anyone else or they can use/misuse your account.

IP – eg: 192.43.87.1
This is really the Net address of a computer; yours. It's always four numbers separated by dots. You may not be given one if your ISP hands them out dynamically when you connect.

DNS – eg 192.43.76.1
Another Net address, this time for the Domain Name Server. The DNS translates human readable Net addresses such as http:/ /www.bbc.com into numbers. This too can be allocated dynamically so you may not need it.

Subnet mask – eg: 255.255.255.0

This is necessary to get you past the server you logged on to and through into the rest of your ISP's local network (and thence to the rest of the Net). You probably won't get one of these.

 With your mail server names, ID and password you can access your e-mail from any computer connected to the Net anywhere in the world, so it's worth keeping this information with you at all times.

Gateway – eg: 192.255.255.255

Yet another Net address though few ISPs require you to specify one. Similar in function to a subnet mask.

Domain – eg: dial.pipex.com

Everyone on the Net is a member of a specific domain. Together with your ID it's used to make up your full e-mail address. It's also often used as part of your Web page address.

SMTP server – eg: smtp.dial.pipex.com

It stands for Simple Mail Transfer Protocol. This is the address of the server which passes on your e-mail when you send it.

POP server – eg: pop.dial.pipex.com

It stands for Post Office Protocol and is the server which looks after e-mail sent to you until you log on and download it.

news server – eg: news.dial.pipex.com

This is the address of the server at your ISP which holds newsgroup postings. You need it to access any newsgroup.

E-mail address – eg: crussell@dial.pipex.com

This is the address to which other people send e-mail intended for you. Many ISPs enable you to create several e-mail addresses for different purposes or users.

Creating a New Connectoid

When you click on Make New Connection in Dial-Up Networking, Windows invokes a wizard which leads you through a series of dialogue boxes each asking for specific information.

This is rapidly becoming the standard way for Windows to request information, and it makes it easy for you.

When you've supplied all the information you get a new icon which Microsoft calls a Connectoid. It has the name you specified.

Clicking on this causes it to dial the number you asked for. This will always work.

However, unless the required Net driver software has been correctly configured with the information it requires, the ISP's modems will simply drop the line again. However, it's useful to be able to test the connectoid.

We'll be coming back to this Connectoid after we've run through setting up the Net driver software.

A new Connectoid appears in Dial-Up Networking.

Pipex (UUnet)

1 Click on Make New Connection and enter a name for your service.

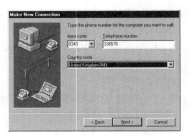

2 The next dialogue box asks for your local access number and country.

3 The final box simply tells you the process is complete. Click Finish.

Setting up Windows Net Drivers

This is the part new PC users find most confusing, but if you work through it logically and enter the information accurately you should have no problems.

Unfortunately, there are slight differences between the dialogue boxes for the original version of Windows 95, the later one and 98, though the principles remain the same. In this section we'll be using the later version of Windows 95 as shipped with new PCs since early in 1997.

First we're going to work through a basic Net set up using the Connection Wizard in Windows. You'll find this on the Programs menu under Accessories, Internet Tools. It also starts automatically the first time you use Internet Explorer or you can run it from the View menu, Internet Options, Connection tab in Internet Explorer.

| Make sure you have all the information you need from your ISP before starting the Internet Connection Wizard. The first screen is an introduction.

2 On the second screen you get various options. To remain in control of the process click on the Manual option. Now you're ready for the good stuff.

3 Another introductory dialogue box appears with a Help option. Check it out to get more detail on the process. When you've read about it click on Next.

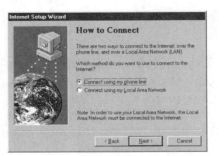

4 Windows now needs to know whether you plan to use a modem. You do. In fact at this stage it should already be installed and correctly set up.

5 The drop down list contains the names of any Connectoid you've set up in Dial-Up Networking. If the right one is already selected click on Next.

6 You may have to enter the phone number again. Next choose United Kingdom from the pull down list and click Bring up Terminal window after dialling.

...cont'd

7 You'll now be asked for your User Name (your ID) and your password. Make sure you enter them both exactly as specified by your ISP.

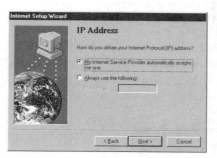

8 Most ISPs dynamically allocate IP addresses (it sends you an IP number for the current session). If not you have to click in the second box and enter yours.

HANDY TIP

Once the information has been entered you can run through the whole thing again as a final check. Windows will show you all the information you entered the first time around.

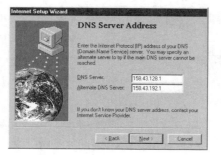

9 DNS is so crucial there's usually more than one. You'll be given them in the order your ISP prefers you to use them. Just enter them accurately.

10 You don't need e-mail to connect to your ISP, but Windows can start setting up Windows messaging to use Net e-mail for you. Click on Next, and that's it!

Entering Information in Network

If you're only using one ISP, and your PC isn't on an internal network – the situation for most home PC users – then you can set up your Net driver software in Network.

To do this you open Control Panel, double click on the Network icon, select TCP/IP from the component list and click on the Properties button.

You'll see a dialogue box with a number of pages. The only ones you're normally interested in are the IP tab and the DNS tab. You can type the information from your ISP straight into this dialogue box.

However, the other useful page here for users of the original Windows 95 is Bindings. Later versions, Windows 95B and 98, automatically bind protocols to adapters, but in the earlier version you have to do this yourself.

The Network applet provides direct access to TCP/IP properties if you're only using one ISP and no other network.

In older versions of Windows 95 you have to explicitly bind the TCP/IP protocol to the Dial-Up Adapter component as shown.

When you set up Net access using an ISP from a Dial-Up Networking connectoid using the Internet Connection Wizard, the settings you enter apply only to that service. If you set them up in Network TCP/IP Properties they apply at all times. Always use the flexible approach.

Troubleshooting your Connection

Don't panic if you can't connect the first time. It's easy to make a mistake or overlook something essential when setting up Net access for the first time.

To fix it, work through the checklist below:

1 Is your modem turned on and connected to the phone socket? Plug a phone into it and listen for a dialling tone.

2 Is your modem connected to your PC using the right cable and the right socket?

3 In Control Panel, open Modems and check the right model is installed. Click Properties and check the COM port is right.

4 Run Dialer from Accessories and try to ring a friend's number using the modem. Tell them what you're doing.

5 If this works, does the ISP's connectoid successfully dial the number of your ISP when you double click it?

6 If you can reach your ISP but it refuses to accept your password check the spelling of your ID and password. The case matters: spatient is not the same as Spatient.

7 You connect to your ISP successfully but can't get anywhere else on the Net. Check the DNS numbers are correct.

8 If you're certain you've done everything right but still can't get connected, phone your ISP's technical support line.

Using your ISP's Net Software

Most ISPs now supply self installing Net access software which handles some or all of the set up for you. To connect you to the Net it must install TCP/IP drivers. It can do this in one of three ways.

TCP/IP drivers are usually called TCP/IP stacks, because they consist of layers of software. An ISP can use a 16-bit or a 32-bit stack. It can further use a Microsoft stack or one from a third party. Under Windows 95/98 it can simply set up the existing 32-bit TCP/IP stack that Microsoft includes. This last option is the preferred one, so it's worth checking.

A 16-bit stack of any kind under Windows 95/98 is a poor deal as it means you can't use 32-bit Windows Net software.

Pipex supplies its own Dial 32-bit software which works well with Windows 95/98. Check with your ISP to make sure you'll be able to run all Windows Net software.

The World Wide Web

The Net owes its current popularity to the World Wide Web, originally shortened to WWW or W3 but now known universally simply as the Web. It was invented by Tim Berners-Lee at the European Cerne Research Centre. In 1991 he bequeathed it to the world where it has become a massive cultural phenomenon that is enjoyed by tens of millions of Net users every day.

Covers

Chapter Three

Introducing the World Wide Web

Effectively, the Web is a collection of electronic documents or pages held on computers around the world. Two things make these pages special: hyperlinks and electronic content.

Hyperlinks are a simple method of enabling a Web page author to provide a link to another Web page anywhere on the Web. All the reader has to do is click on the link to be taken to another page, wherever it's located on the Net.

Web pages are written using a simple text based mark up language called HTML (HyperText Markup Language). Web pages can include text, images, sounds and most other kinds of digital content.

Web pages always support full colour and, unlike printed pages, can be interactive. They can even be made to recognise you and present information tailored to your particular requirements.

Recently, there's been a trend toward more interactive web pages using programs written in one of two ways – Java and ActiveX. Some browsers don't support them.

The World Wide Web is brought to you by a Net protocol called HTTP (Hypertext Transfer Protocol). The software you need for HTTP is a Web browser. We're using Microsoft Internet Explorer to demonstrate the Web, though there are other browsers available, most notably Netscape's Communicator.

No one has any real idea how many Web pages there are. They're created by individuals, companies, organisations, and anyone else who wants to publish them. Your ISP provides free Web space where you too can join the free global electronic publishing bonanza and add your own offering to the hundreds of millions of pages on hundreds of thousands of Web sites.

What enables it to work is the unique Net address possessed by every Web page on the Net. We'll take a look at these and see how they're constructed.

The URL – How Net Addresses Work

The proper name for a Web page address is a URL, which stands for Uniform Resource Locator. Although written in one piece each URL actually consists of four basic parts: [net protocol][domain name][path][page name]

Let's examine a real life example:

In general, the first part of a URL isn't case sensitive, though it's unusual not to type in lower case when using URLs. However, the path and file name can be case sensitive, so if you're given a URL with capital letters in it then use them exactly as shown.

The first part is **http:** which is the protocol. It finishes with a double colon and is separated from the next part by two forward slashes. The same approach is used for **ftp:** and other protocols apart from **news:**, which doesn't have the forward slash separators for historical reasons.

Next is the domain: **www.bt.co.uk** (the Web site run by BT. British Telecom owns this domain name. No one else can use it). A DNS computer looks this up and translates it into a real, four-number Net address.

The third section starts after the first single forward slash (**/home/**). It describes the folder path to the required page on the computer being used as a Web server.

The final part is the file name of the Web page. In this example it's **index.htm.** The first and last items of a Net address are often defaults – **www.bt.co.uk/home/** works perfectly well with most modern browsers. The browser assumes the **http://** prefix and the Web server hands out an index.htm page automatically if another isn't specified. This is common practice, though the default page name varies from one ISP and server to another.

Because the Web is designed to be simple to use you can often guess the URL of a company or organisation. For example, if you were looking for the BBC's site you might try typing in **www.bbc.com** or **www.bbc.co.uk**. It can be surprisingly simple to track down a Web address and get on to the site. Then hyperlinks are all you need.

Understanding Web Browsers

Modern web browsers are extremely flexible and configurable. You can change the way the toolbars look and even whether or not they're present. Computer Step offer books on both major browsers: Internet Explorer and Netscape Communicator. The Help systems attached to each are also worth looking through.

Web address of the current Web page (URL).

The icons at the top are for the main services. These include Back and Forward to visit pages, Stop and Print.

Links to places the browser vendor believes you will want to go. You can normally turn off this toolbar.

The content window is the place where pages are displayed. This BT page has an interactive form.

Horizontal and vertical scroll bars for large pages.

The status bar displays page download progress and the URL of links under the cursor.

The basic operation and default settings of all current Web browsers are fairly sensible, which means you can use it just as it is after installing it. It's worth familiarising yourself with it before attempting to change the way it works.

Which Web Browser?

There are two major Web browser vendors of interest to the home user: Netscape and Microsoft. Despite what their various marketing departments claim, the browsers are fairly evenly matched and either will do a great job for you.

The only major limitation on Netscape Navigator (the browser that comes as part of the Communicator suite) is its inability to run Microsoft's ActiveX applets.

There are, though, other browsers available. Perhaps the most famous is Mosaic. This is still fairly common in commercial environments. In general, only the two major browsers come close to supporting all the instructions and multimedia types used on current Web sites.

In this book we've chosen to use Internet Explorer. This is because it works well with Windows 95/98 and is available (at the time of writing – things change fast in the world of the Net) for free. You can get it from www.microsoft.com/ie.

As you can see, the basic layout of Netscape Navigator is remarkably similar to that of Internet Explorer. Either will do perfectly well for most Web sites.

If you plan to buy a TV set-top box for Net access there are one or two potential problems of which you should be aware. Not all of them have Web browsers capable of handling the majority of Web pages, which means you either won't be able to see them or they will appear broken.

The other problem is TV itself. It has a low resolution compared with a computer monitor, and Web pages are designed for high resolution monitors. It can prove impossible to display them on TV. Start with a PC to see how it *should* work.

Installing your Web Browser

If you've bought a new PC it will come with Microsoft Internet Explorer pre-installed on it. However, you may want to install a newer version or to install Netscape Communicator instead.

The first thing you have to do is get hold of the browser itself. There are two main sources of new free and trial software, including Web browsers.

The first is from the Web site of the software vendor concerned and the second is from computer magazine cover mounted CD-ROMs. Both are effective methods of distribution.

Modern browser suites are big though; files more than 10Mb in size are common. These can take a long time to download, but you'll always get the latest version.

Installing the new browser is no harder than installing any other software. It will come with a Setup.exe file. Double click on it and away it goes.

For simplicity, it's easiest to accept all the defaults and install everything on offer.

Competition on the Net is intense and this encourages vendors to rush software out before it's really ready. If you install the latest versions of browsers, and other Net software, expect to put up with bugs and missing features.

Both Internet Explorer and Netscape Navigator are best left to install themselves unless you're a Net expert.

Configuring your Browser

This is a large and fairly personal subject, so we're going to hit the high points simply, to show you the kind of things you can change to make them work the way you want them to work. The location and often the name of specific preference settings varies but the basic features are present in most browsers.

From the View menu you have access to the two main browser configuration options. The first is the Toolbars option, the second is the last entry – Internet Options.

Changing Internet Options

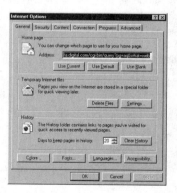

From here you can change the default Home Page visited when the browser starts. You can alter the cache settings for temporary files and access History settings (pages you've visited recently). You can also alter browser colours, fonts, language and the accessibility options.

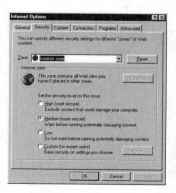

The Security tab enables you to specify sites you'll accept active content from – content such as programs embedded in a Web page – and those that you won't. In practice, for Dial-Up users the default security settings are sensible.

The Content tab provides access to the Content Advisor – don't Enable it or you won't be able to access 99.9 per cent of the Web. Certificates don't work well and Personal Info is for keeping encrypted credit card details handy for Net shopping.

You shouldn't normally have to worry about the Connection tab. It's aimed more at those with complex local network and Internet access in companies. However, you can also run the Internet Connection Wizard from here.

HANDY TIP

If you don't understand what a preference setting is for, don't alter it. If you must alter it take a note of what it was before in case it doesn't do quite what you expect.

On the Programs tab you'll find options to set the default programs you want to use for e-mail and newsgroup access as well as your addressing options. 'Internet Explorer should check to see whether it is the default browser' is a way for Microsoft to stay in control.

The Advanced tab has the multimedia check boxes you need to turn off automatic playing of video, sound and animations – all of which slow Web pages dramatically. The others are best left alone for the time being.

Types of Web Site

As stated earlier, no one owns the Net, or the Web, though every Web site belongs to someone or some organisation. The kind of site it is depends on who created it and why. This may sound obvious, but once you start looking the Web can appear confused and without purpose.

One way to think about the Web is as a single giant magazine. Newsstand magazines each have a target audience. It's obvious who each is aimed at. The Web can be harder to fathom at first. It can seem as if you've bought one magazine three miles thick with no contents page.

Later, you'll find out how to use search engines to locate the kind of site you want, but first we're going to look at examples of the main types of Web site.

Institutional sites

http://www.brent.gov.uk/brent/other/uklg/uklgtype.htm#emet

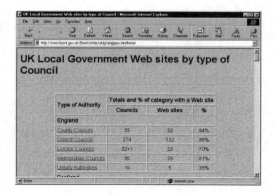

Most Government departments, local authorities and the various QUANGOs with which the UK abounds have their own Web sites. These are often out of date and dull looking but make a good starting point for information about a locale, local opportunities, contact information and so on. This list of local authority sites is maintained by Brent council.

ISP sites

http://www.dial.pipex.com/

ISPs all have Web sites. These carry information on pricing, support, downloadable software and other useful information for Dial-Up users. They also tend to provide a fast access point for personal Web pages held on the ISP's servers.

Sales sites

http://www.amazon.com

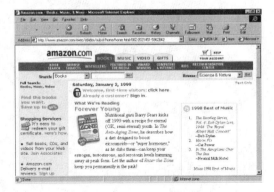

Sales sites, also called e-commerce sites, are basically on-line shops selling everything from insurance to groceries. The most successful specialise: Dell in PCs, Amazon in books, and so on. A new phenomena (at the time of writing) is the on-line megastore where you can buy just about anything.

News sites

http://www.telegraph.co.uk

Many people thought news would be a compelling use of the Web, though in practice it didn't turn out that way. However, all the major newspapers and many magazines have Web sites which are maintained largely as a come-on. Check them out.

Sex sites

http://www.sexmuseum.com/

Sex sites are the most successful site category on the Net, accounting for 20 per cent of Net usage and, by some estimates, 25 per cent of all Net commerce. Most, like this one, require membership fees before you can look at the good (or bad) stuff.

Company sites

http://www.pace.co.uk/

One day all companies will have Net addresses just as they all have fax numbers. The trend started with communications and computer companies but now extends to any business capable of selling beyond its immediate geographical area.

Personal sites

http://www.44calibre.co.uk/gnr/gunsnroses.html

The Web has made it possible for everyone to publish on-line at a tiny cost. Such Web sites range from simple contact information to baroque shrines dedicated to a personal interest. Some of the best Web sites are labours of love.

Finding Web Sites Again

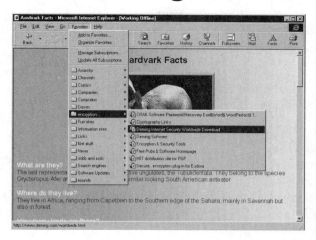

With millions of Web sites available it's easy to find yourself on a site you'd like to visit again. Sure, you could write down the URL but there's a better way.

Internet Explorer and Netscape Navigator will remember the Web address for you using Favourites and Bookmarks respectively. They work in the same way so we'll use Favourites as an example.

Adding Favourites

Click a radio button to determine how the site will be remembered. The sensible default is to simply add it as a Favourite.

The default name is the page title but you can call it anything you like.

Use the Create In button to choose a folder for the site.

Use the New Folder button to make folders for Favourites.

The Create In button opens the lower pane which shows an Explorer style view of your Favourites folders.

Off-line Browsing

Using Web pages off-line – when you're not connected to the Net – is much cheaper than doing so on-line. All the major browsers have off-line browsing but Internet Explorer is the most flexible with three ways to do it. From the File menu click on Work Off-Line first.

It may seem obvious, but you won't be able to view any Web page off-line unless it's first downloaded when you're on-line. However, if a page is missing from the cache you will be asked if you want to go on-line and retrieve it.

1 Use Channels: a new feature of the Net which may turn out to be the standard method of delivering entertainment on-line. The feature is supported in Internet Explorer and Netscape Communicator.

2 Subscribe to any Web site: once a site has been made a Favourite you can choose to subscribe to it. It's then

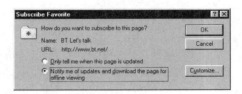

automatically checked and any changes downloaded whenever you log on. Use sparingly as it can lead to a lot of unwanted downloads. Subscribed sites are always saved and won't be deleted in the same way as old cache entries.

3 Use the History list: you'll find this on the View menu. Choose Explorer Bar and then History. This adds a list of recently visited sites. Click on one and it's displayed if it's in the cache on the hard drive.

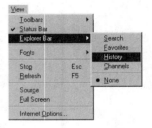

Using Search Engines

The Web is essentially a random collection of pages with no over-arching organisation, merely hyperlinks. However, by following all the links you should be able to reach every publicly accessible page on the Web. Several companies have automated this process and created Web page indexes which you can use to locate Web pages containing material you may find interesting.

Some companies, most notably Yahoo, also try to catalogue the Web. This has to be done by hand but produces results which, in some circumstances, are more useful. However, while automatic indexing eventually pulls in most pages, a lot less of the Web gets catalogued.

Finally, there's the ongoing problem of ghost pages. Links are a one way thing. If the page goes the link remains; it simply doesn't lead anywhere. This also applies to search engines which will often have pages indexed which no longer exist. Estimates put the number of links to ghost pages at anything up to 20 per cent of all the links on the Web. Frustrating, but then 80 per cent work.

Search engine addresses

http://www.altavista.com/
http://www.excite.com/
http://www.lycos.com/
http://www.infoseek.com/
http://www.webcrawler.com/

Web catalogue addresses

http://www.yahoo.com/
http://www.yell.co.uk/

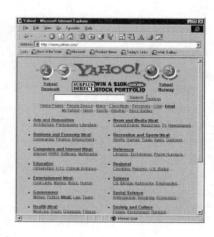

Yahoo was the first and it remains the best of the on-line Web site catalogues.

When you construct a query for a search engine you need to be fairly precise. Single words, unless extremely specialised, will produce hundreds of thousands of hits (pages containing the word). To reduce this to a useful list you need to refine your search. All search engines enable you to do this but the syntax used varies. So the first thing to do is check the help page for the search engine and print out the instructions for creating an effective query. Let's take a look at the kind of query you can construct at Altavista, one of the best Web search engines available.

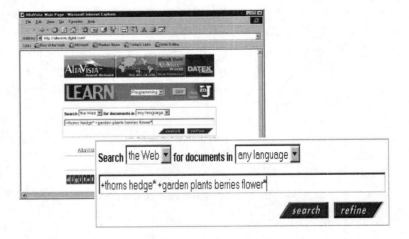

We're looking for a thorny garden hedging plant, so thorns and garden have a plus sign in front of them to show the words must be in the pages on the result list.

2 Even this fairly refined search produced more than 11,000 hits so we had to tighten it up a little more. This reduced it to a few hundred more useful links, including this one.

Browser Plug-ins and Dynamic HTML

Some Web page data types (music or graphics in unusual formats for example) aren't directly supported by browsers. They require another program called a Helper applet in Internet Explorer or a Plug-in in Netscape Communicator.

As Netscape Communicator (and its Navigator component) are intended to run on a variety of computers with different operating systems, almost all support for data formats is provided by plug-ins, although many of these are effectively built into the browser. Check the Netscape site at **http://www.netscape.com** for details of available plug-ins.

Internet Explorer is largely aimed at a Windows computing environment and basically supports all the data types Windows itself supports, so it doesn't make much use of plug-ins. You do, though, need different kinds of plug-ins for browsers from different vendors.

If a Web page says it needs a specific plug-in to work properly it will usually carry a link to the plug-in. Check the link and see if there are versions for your browser.

If a Web page appears broken don't assume the problem is at your end. Unless the opening page tells you it needs a specific browser or plug-in it's probably really broken.

Dynamic HTML

The latest Web page feature is called Dynamic HTML – DHTML for short. This enables Web page authors to make better looking pages with far more user interaction than previously without necessarily resorting to embedded Java or ActiveX applets – though it will probably have the opposite effect in practice.

Even more unfortunate, it isn't a standard as yet and the support for the two versions built into Microsoft and Netscape's browsers are currently completely incompatible.

In practice this means you either install both browsers and use whichever one the dynamic Web site specifies or you ignore sites you can't read with your favourite browser.

Java and ActiveX Explained

Java is the name of a programming language invented at computer company Sun. It's designed to be machine independent, which means Java programs can run on any computer.

For them to do this the computer must have a special program running called a Java Virtual Machine. This is a program that thinks it's a computer. Any real computer with a JVM available can run Java programs.

The most common use for Java to date is in Web pages. Netscape and Microsoft support Java in their browsers.

ActiveX is Microsoft's extension of its Windows software technology to Web pages. Only Microsoft's browser will run ActiveX programs. However, on Windows systems ActiveX works much better than Java – and there are more than 100 million Windows PCs, whereas all the non-Windows computers together come to only 20 million or so, so ActiveX is clearly not going to go away.

 Both ActiveX and Java enable a Web page author to deliver a program to your PC and run it automatically. This poses obvious security risks, which is why all browsers enable you to turn off Java (and ActiveX in Internet Explorer) support. Some sites won't work without one or other of these. You have to decide for yourself whether or not to trust these programs. There can be no guarantees.

Java programs are implemented as classes. So for example, a program to play noughts and crosses might be called: **noughtandcross.class**

ActiveX programs are technically a Windows OCX component so the above program might become: **noughtandcross.ocx**

There is also a scripting version of Java called JavaScript and a separate scripting language supported by Internet Explorer called Visual Basic Script.

These can be written directly into a Web page as text and don't need to be turned into a program applet first. Internet Explorer runs some JavaScripts and VB Scripts but Netscape Navigator only runs JavaScripts. Both run slowly compared with the applets.

E-mail

One of the great things the Internet allows us to do is to communicate with one another.

In pre-Internet days the regular postal service was the way the majority of people kept in touch with one another. Today, however, the Net provides us with an electronic alternative which is much quicker and just as easy to use.

Covers

Chapter Four

All about E-mail

E-mail is probably the most fundamental of all the services available over the Internet.

It accounts for the bulk of Net usage worldwide and is used by more netizens than any other service. Oh, and it's fast and simple too.

It works in pretty much the same way as ordinary mail (known as snail mail to the jargon fiends because of its speed in comparison to its electronic equivalent). The sender simply starts up a special e-mail program and types in his or her message. The next step is to add the e-mail address of the intended recipient, or recipients, and finally it's necessary to hit the magic 'send' button.

Provided the machine is connected to the Internet at the time, the e-mail program will automatically send the message anywhere in the world in an instant.

It is the speed that makes the major difference between traditional mail and e-mail. Where ordinary postboxes are only emptied three or four times a day and their contents delivered the following day at best, the Internet never sleeps. E-mail is electronically collected every few seconds from special on-line mailing centres and even messages destined for the opposite side of the globe can be flashed over there in a moment. Indeed, in some instances it is possible to carry out almost 'real-time' conversations with friends and colleagues thousands of miles away.

The second great advantage of e-mail of course is in the cost. To send a first class inland letter in the UK can be expensive; to send bulky documents, even more so. Sending the same message in electronic format takes only a few seconds and many telephone companies charge a maximum of five or ten pence for three minutes. It's also possible to send the same e-mail to any number of friends - hundreds if you have them! The beauty of such mass mailing is that the message only needs to be typed once. Beware however: mass e-mailing lots of people you don't know is frowned upon (see chapter seven for more details).

Use Outlook Express

There are many e-mail packages available for the Net user and to a great degree they all perform the same duties. Some, however, stand out above the rest and Microsoft's Outlook Express – which is available as part of the Internet Explorer suite/Windows 98 – has some truly wonderful features.

Download Outlook Express as part of the IE4/IE5 package from http://www.microsoft.com/ie/

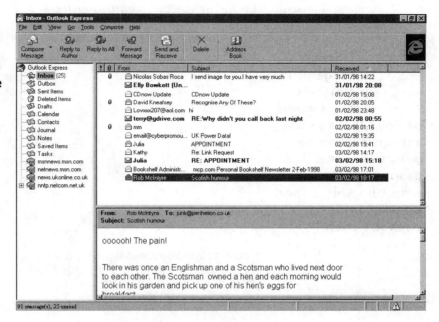

One of Outlook's great strengths is in its features list. These range from creating simple text-only mail messages to HTML-rich documents; the creation of custom mail lists which allow one message to be sent to a host of different recipients; filtering to stop "spam" mail; even allowing graphics or program files to be attached to messages and sent anywhere in the world.

Over the next few pages we'll look at how to set up and use Outlook Express, but the techniques and methods described will be equally at home when applied to most e-mail programs.

Setting up your E-mail

Setting up your e-mail program is not a difficult task to achieve, but before you begin it's advisable to collect a few details.

Start with your e-mail address and while you're at it, check with your mail account provider (usually the organisation with whom you have your dial-up account) for the details of incoming and outgoing mail servers.

With those details safely written down follow these steps :

Don't forget to find out the details of your ISP's e-mail server, as well as your username and password. You won't be able to set up your mail without them!

1 Outlook Express starts by asking for your full name.

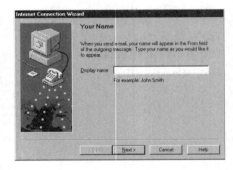

2 Next, provide your e-mail address in the box provided.

3 Now it's time to refer to the details you took down from your provider. Most e-mail accounts today operate from POP3 servers, but it doesn't harm to check.

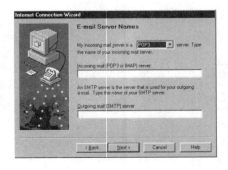

4 The username and password for the mail account is entered next. Only select the Secure Password option if your provider tells you it's necessary.

5 Outlook Express now lets you choose a special name for your mail account (useful if you have several of them).

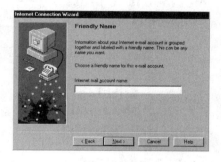

6 Selecting option 1 will start your connection every time you start Outlook. Option 2 is useful if your PC is part of a Local Area Network whilst option 3 is for those who spend time reading mail offline and don't want to be hassled by dial-up dialogue boxes.

7 Hoorah! All done, now all you need is some e-mail to deal with ...

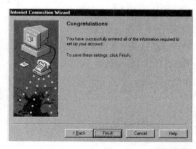

Sending E-mail

Sending e-mail is easy. Start by selecting the Compose Message icon at the top left of the Outlook window, or by Selecting the New Message option in the Compose menu.

 The quickest way to open a new message is to press Control-N.

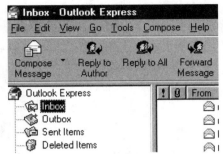

 Clicking the small arrow next to Compose Message allows the use of special E-mail forms called stationary - more on this later in the chapter.

1 Type the e-mail address of the recipient here.

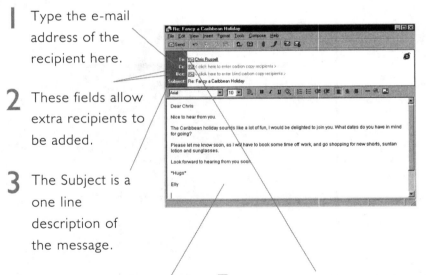

2 These fields allow extra recipients to be added.

3 The Subject is a one line description of the message.

 Using the Outlook Express Address Book makes it easier to address messages to regular contacts and friends.

4 The body of the message is entered here.

5 Click the Send button when the message is complete.

Replying to a Message

Sooner or later it is necessary to write back to someone who has sent you a message.

By highlighting the message in the Received Mail pane then clicking Reply To Author you can send a message back without the need to retype the details of the person you are replying to.

Using reply also means you can quote portions of the original message for message clarity.

Outlook automatically fills in the recipient's name and quotes the original message title, adding Re: to show it's a response.

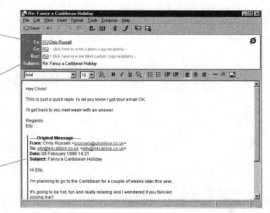

BEWARE

Quoting a whole message when only giving a short reply can be annoying. Always try to cut out parts of the original E-mail which are not relevant to things you are commenting on.

The original text is marked off with a thick line or ">" symbol to differentiate it from the reply.

Attaching Files

Attaching huge files to your outgoing messages means your mail will take longer to send and may upset the recipient unless you have warned them first!

Not all e-mail messages contain plain text and sometimes it's desirable to send program files, graphics or even sounds to someone as part of an e-mail.

Because of the complex way in which e-mails are sent around the Net it's not always possible to embed them directly into a message. Instead, they need to be sent as attachments to the text part of the message.

Almost anything can be attached to an e-mail, but if you are going to send files in obscure formats to your friends or colleagues be sure to check they have software which can understand those formats.

Some ISPs will not let you send big attachments. ße sure to check if there's a limit on e-mail size.

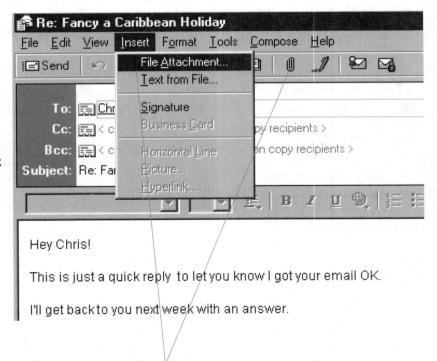

You can attach files by selecting the File Attachment option of the Insert menu or by clicking on the paperclip icon in the toolbar.

Once the attachment option has been chosen, a file selection box pops up. To attach the file, simply find it on your computer and then click the attach button. Outlook Express will do any necessary encoding and then send it for you automatically.

I Select the file(s) you wish to attach using this dialogue box.

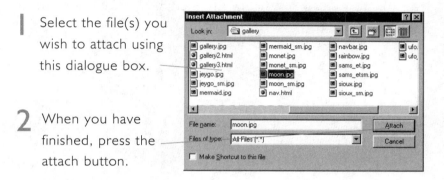

2 When you have finished, press the attach button.

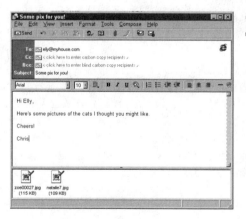

3 Files which have been attached to email messages appear in the bar at the bottom of the window. Outlook helpfully gives you the size of each file too.

Formatting your Mail

Sending e-mail to friends and contacts around the globe can be a tremendously rewarding and exciting experience, but let's face it, sending plain text is a little dull...

It's a good job then that Outlook Express (and some other commonly available mail packages) allow you to send "rich" e-mail which contains images and even HTML codes to help the message stand out from the crowd.

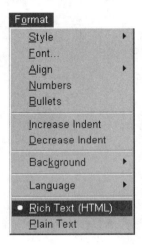

Using Outlook Express it's first necessary to open up a Reply or New Message window. Next, move the cursor to the Format option and make sure the Rich Text (HTML) option has a black dot next to it (this indicates Rich Text mode is already on).

Clicking on Plain Text will only allow you to enter letters and numbers in your message. This is sometimes useful if you know you're sending e-mail to someone who cannot handle formatted text messages.

If in doubt, check before sending.

With Rich Text in force your Reply/New Message window will have the following bar across the top of it, allowing you to set different fonts, typesizes (useful for making a point or if you're writing to someone with a sight problem), horizontal rules, and even add pictures to make your mail that bit brighter.

Include hyperlinks and pictures here

Change typeface and size here

Text colours and styles may be set here

Outlook also provides a special set of e-mail templates called stationery, which you may use for special occasions. You can even create your own for everyday use.

Stationery is available from the Compose menu, by clicking on the New Message Using... option. After selecting this you are presented with a handful of options covering a number of celebratory events ranging from birthdays to baby news and holiday announcements.

REMEMBER **If you're sending mail to someone who doesn't use Outlook Express they may not be able to see your artistic talents.**

Clicking on the More Stationery option opens up a dialogue box with 20 different kinds of stationery to choose from. When you've found the one you like just select it and a new message will be opened automatically with the chosen Paper displayed in the message composition window. Just choosing No Stationery will give you a plain white background.

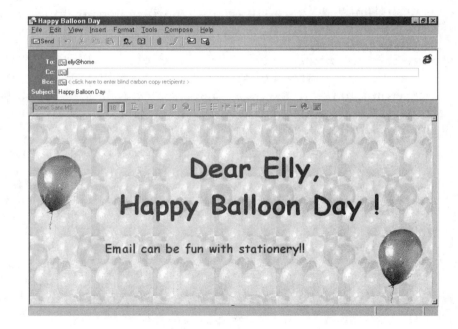

Filtering your Messages

If you subscribe to a large number of mailing lists or have a lot of friends who mail you every day, you'll soon discover that e-mail can build up very quickly into a disorganised electronic heap of messages.

You can, of course, create individual folders for your mail, dedicated to particular subjects or correspondents, and go through every message which arrives, carefully filing each in the right place.

Or you can make use of mail filtering to do all of the hard work for you.

Mail filtering is a very efficient way of organising your messages but care must be taken to ensure messages are not accidentally deleted or filed into the wrong mail folders. Check your rules carefully!

Filtering relies on the mailbox owner setting up a series of rules which the e-mail package uses when deciding what to do with each message.

For example, all messages from Demon Internet users might be placed straight into an appropriate folder, whilst mail relating to your job goes into a second and messages from your favourite cat mailing list are passed to a third.

Such is the power of mail filtering that messages can even be examined and deleted from mail servers before they are downloaded – a great help in wasting time downloading spam (see chapter 7 on Netiquette for more about Spam).

Setting up the rules for filtering may sound like a complicated task but if you follow these simple steps you'll have it all sorted out in no time.

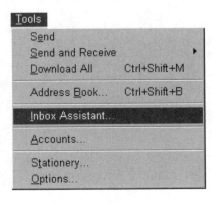

The first stage is to select the Inbox Assistant from the Tools menu. It is here that the rules which govern mail filtering can be set up.

...cont'd

1 Select which
messages to
filter by address,
subject, the
account to
which they are
sent or by size.

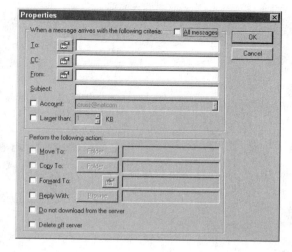

2 This section
defines what
action is to be
taken with messages which meet the criteria specified above.
Note that Delete off Server will destroy the message before
you get to read it.

Using this dialogue box, any number of filtering rules can
be defined and applied to messages which pass through the
program. Once you've finished, Outlook Express will
display the rules currently in place for easy reference.

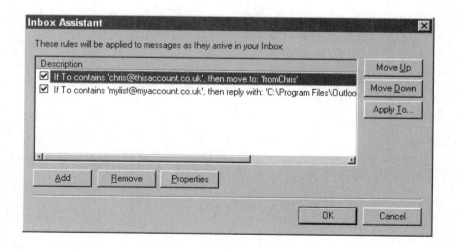

Maintaining an Address Book

There's nothing worse than sitting down to write a quick message to a friend and then discovering you've forgotten their e-mail address.

To prevent this from happening, many mail packages provide a snazzy little address book. Take a look at Outlook's offering:

Start by clicking the Address Book button on the Outlook menu bar.

Highlight a name in the list then click here to send an e-mail.

2 The Address book opens up, showing two entries so far.

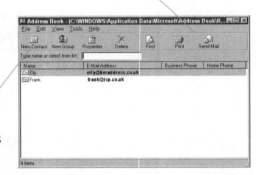

Use this button to collect contact names into handy groups.

3 Clicking on properties gives you all of the details for a contact.

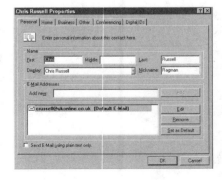

Signing Your Messages

If you've ever noticed how some people have witty or informative messages at the bottom of their missives then you've already seen an e-mail signature.

The signature is a simple but very effective way of getting a message across to everyone you e-mail.

Whether it's the URL of your web site, your e-mail address, or even just a comedy motto of the month, the signature can be used to portray any message.

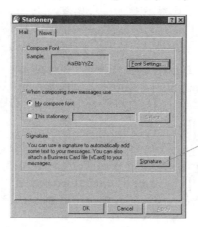

Select the Stationery option from the Tools menu then click here to create your own signature.

Click this box to attach your signature to all of the messages you send.

This is the signature itself; include anything you like here.

Virtual business cards may not display properly in all e-mail packages, so don't rely on them.

Set up your own details in the Address Book (see facing page) and then select them here. Outlook will send a Virtual Business Card containing your phone number (etc) with each mail you send.

Online and Offline Reading

In spite of all its advantages and the fact that sending e-mails can be much cheaper than using the conventional mail service, e-mail can in the long run be quite expensive.

The reason for this is quite simple – many people get into the habit of staying online while reading their mail and composing their replies. If there is a lot of mail to answer (or you're simply a slow typist) this can mean the phone bill will soon mount up.

Thankfully the bulk of modern mail readers can operate in two different modes, online and offline, as an aid to those people trying to keep the phone bills down.

In online mode the mail program will allow the creation of e-mail messages. When the Send button is pressed it will automatically send the message(s) to their intended destination.

In offline mode, messages can be created but when the Send is pressed the e-mails are copied into the Outbox where they are held until the user dials up to the Net and presses the Send & Receive button.

It is not necessary to be online to handle your e-mail and in many cases it is preferable to be offline as it gives more time to consider what is being written and the way in which it is being written.

In other instances, online e-mail can be a real advantage. If, for example, you're on holiday and want to keep in touch with events at home, online e-mail is a much cheaper way to communicate than making very expensive long distance phone calls. Assuming you have access to a computer it's possible to get hold of your mail and read it in seconds for the price of a local call – wherever you happen to be.

However, the majority of Internet Service Providers in the UK don't provide their customers with the facilities to read and respond to mail from anywhere in the world which leaves the electronic traveller in a bit of a jam.

Help is at hand, however, from companies such as HotMail in the USA and Digital Mail here in the UK.

Both companies provide special interfaces to mailboxes which can be viewed through a web browser. This means that e-mail can be viewed from anywhere in the world (assuming you have access to a computer that is).

For more information visit:

http://www.hotmail.com

http://www.digitalmail.com

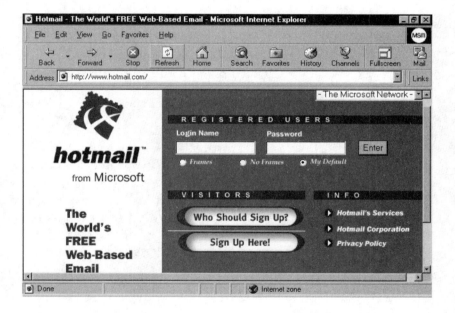

Other E-mail Packages

In this chapter we've based all of the examples around Microsoft's Outlook Express.

There are of course plenty of others available and some of them, like Outlook, are totally free.

If you don't fancy using the Microsoft package try any of these for size:

Calypso 32 – http://www.mcsdallas.com/

DTS mail 32 – http://dtsoftware.simplenet.com/

Eudora lite – http://www.eudora.com/eudoralight/

Pegasus Mail – http://www.pegasus.usa.com/

Internet Explorer (or Windows 98) and Netscape Communicator provide browsers, newsreaders, e-mail programs and more in one neat, free package.

Microsoft Internet Explorer – http://www.microsoft.com/ie

Netscape Communicator – http://www.netscape.com

It is interesting (if not necessarily surprising) to note that the most popular e-mail packages on the net outside of Internet Explorer and Netscape Communicator are also both totally free. Copies of Pegasus and Eudora Lite are available from the addresses above and provide excellent ways of accessing your mail.

Newsgroups

With the exception of e-mail, probably the greatest use of the Internet for interpersonal communication is through the newsgroups.

In this chapter we'll take an in-depth look at what the newsgroups are, how they work and how you can connect up to them and chat with like-minded individuals on more than 20,000 different topics.

Covers

What are Newsgroups?

In the early days of the Internet, e-mail was the king of the communication methods. It was (and still is) quick, easy to use and everyone with an Internet connection had it set up as standard.

But there was a problem with it.

E-mail relies entirely on the fact that everyone within a particular discussion group or circle of friends can remember everyone else's e-mail address – not a big task if there are only a handful of close friends or colleagues talking-over a project for example, but what happens if it's desirable to open the subject to anyone that happens to be passing by?

By the late 1970s two students from Duke University in the United States hit upon the answer. Rather than relying on the one-to-one communication method that was e-mail they built a system which provided one-to-many communication.

The idea was that by connecting together a series of Internet servers designed to handle the message traffic for the system, called Usenet, every message from everyone taking part could be stored centrally – exactly like using an old fashioned notice or bulletin board. The great advantage of this system of working was that individual areas, or groups, could be created at will to handle conversations on any matter that came to mind: so there would be a home for the computer scientists, one for business people and even one for those who wished to chat about the weather or the price of beans at their local supermarket (this is not as ridiculous as it sounds – read on and discover later in this chapter just how silly things can get!).

From humble and rather tentative beginnings the system of newsgroups grew swiftly to the point today where there are more than 25,000 publicly accessible groups available at the push of a button.

The sheer volume of groups made the process of keeping tabs on the news service a virtually impossible task. To make things easier, the Usenet administrators introduced a hierarchical structure which ordered the groups into categories.

In essence there are seven major content areas each of which contain many thousands of sub groups.

The major areas are:

alt.* – An unusual category which holds "alternative" newsgroups. From discussions on the mental health of the Muppets' Swedish Chef to juggling techniques.

comp.* – Groups within this category are technical and/or computer related. From the greenest of beginners to networking experts, everyone is welcome to drop in here and have their say.

misc.* – Covering subjects ranging from jobs to marital problems, there's a little bit of everything in the misc. hierarchy.

news.* – An Internet-related group which gives the latest news and information on breaking stories, updates on Net abuses and all you need to know on software releases and more. A great place to start for Net beginners.

rec.* – The Internet's favourite recreational chat area. From sports fans to couch potatoes there are groups in here to cater for every taste (and it's a Star Trek fan's paradise!).

sci.* – If it ends in "ology" you'll find it here. Science theory, fact and fiction rub shoulders within the sci. hierarchy.

soc.* – Groups relating to cultures and societies across the globe can be found in here.

New areas, complete with their own groups are springing up every day so keep a sharp eye out for them.

Configuring your Newsreader

There are many different programs available across the Internet which are designed to enable access to the newsgroups.

Some must be paid for, others are given away as shareware and a percentage are even given away free.

For the sake of this section of the chapter we'll be using the Outlook Express package to demonstrate how it's done but as with the last chapter, the information and methods used here are equally applicable to most newsgroup packages.

Outlook Express starts by asking for your e-mail address so people can respond directly as well as through the newsgroups.

2 The next step is to provide details of your ISP's news server. Usually this will be in the form news.yourisp.co.uk or similar but it's best to check. If your news server requires you to enter your username and password you should click the box at the bottom of the page.

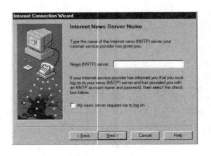

3 Provide Outlook Express with a suitable name which describes the news connection (for example "Demon news account").

4 This dialogue box
allows you to control
the way
in which Outlook
Express connects to
the Internet.

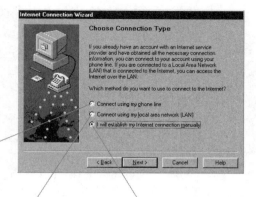

The program will dial
up for you every time
you launch Outlook
Express.

This option is designed
to be used by those
connected to existing
Intranets with Internet
capabilities.

The final option is most
useful for those who
prefer to access their
mail after dialing-up using
a separate program (like
a dial-up networking
connection.

5 Congratulations!
Your newsreader is
now ready to go.

The News Server

If you followed the steps in the previous section you should be just about ready to "surf" your way through the many thousands of available groups.

Before you do there's one final step that needs to be taken, and that's to connect the news server and download a list of all of the available groups.

It's important to note that not all ISPs provide full and complete Usenet news feeds. There may be many reasons for this, the main reason being censorship at present – some ISPs block groups with content which may provide legal problems in this country. Legality is only one issue, however, and there may be many other reasons why particular groups are not available.

HANDY TIP

If your ISP doesn't provide a newsgroup you are interested in, mail the newsmaster and ask them to give you access – most will be happy to help.

Questions of legality and morality aside, the news server acts as a huge coordinating computer communicating with hundreds of similar machines across the globe to ensure everything is kept as up-to-date as possible so that participants and lurkers (those who read but don't participate in the on-going chats) can keep up-to-date.

This coordination process is a two part operation as the list of active newsgroups needs to be maintained in addition to the list of active messages within each group.

Due to the high volume of message traffic through Usenet it is not uncommon to find that some older messages in certain newsgroups will be unavailable even a relatively short time after they were originally posted. However, if this happens there's no need to despair, as search engines exist which can find particular messages for you if required (more on this facility later in this chapter).

In the first instance, you'll probably find there's plenty of existing information to satisfy your curiosity. The easiest way to find it is to narrow your search down to a target set of newsgroups and then browse around until you discover what it is that you are looking for.

With Outlook Express the easiest way to do this is by first clicking on the name of the news server you wish to access, followed by the Newsgroups button in the menu bar at the top of the screen.

BEWARE

Down-loading a list of newsgroups for the first time may take a while (there are currently more than 25,000).

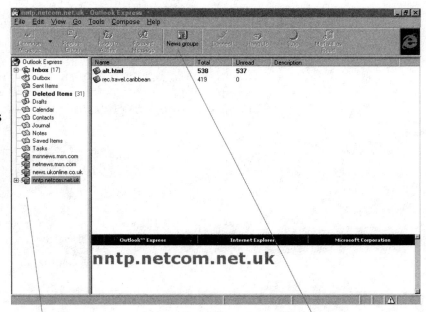

Clicking on any of these server icons gives access to the appropriate news server.

Selecting this option will pop up Outlook's newsgroup selection box for the selected server (see below).

All available servers are listed here.

The newsgroups are listed here.

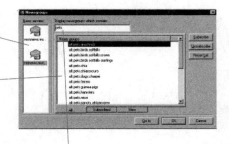

If a word, or part-word is entered here, Outlook will find matching newsgroups.

Subscribing to Newsgroups

With the newsreader set up and all of the available group names downloaded onto your machine it's time to browse around and see what's out there in the wide world of Usenet.

Taking a look is one thing, but suppose you come across a really interesting group which concentrates on British comedy and you want to subscribe to that group so you can go back again and again to see what's happening.

Unlike subscribing to printed publications, subs to Usenet newsgroups are free (with some rare exceptions) and all it takes is a couple of clicks of the mouse button to subscribe.

Click the Newsgroups button to bring up the list of available groups.

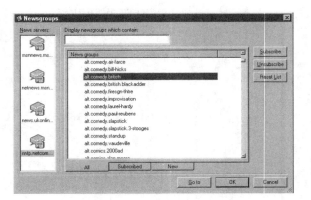

2 Highlight the group that's of interest to you and then press the subscribe button.

3 A small newspaper icon appears next to your chosen group. Click the OK button to finish (clicking Go To will take you straight to the newsgroup).

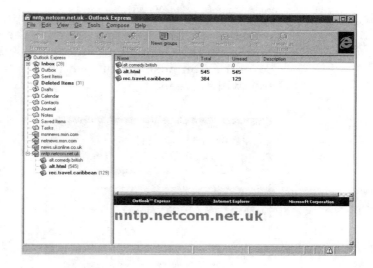

4 Outlook automatically adds the group to your existing subscriptions list and even tells you how many messages there are and how many you've read.

Postings Explained

The heart of the newsgroups lies, of course, in the messages which are posted there. Without the input of the newsgroup users the whole system would quickly fall into disrepair.

To this end it's vitally important, and great fun, to throw your own comments and messages into the Usenet melting pot.

In essence, posting to Usenet is just as simple as sending an e-mail message.

After finding an appropriate group into which to post your message it's first necessary to click the Compose message button on the Outlook menu bar (or select New message from the Compose menu), which will bring forward the following screen:

1 Fill-in the name of the group you wish to post into here.

2 A suitable subject line should go here. The subject is a one line summary of what your posting is all about.

3 The text of the posting goes here.

4 When everything is OK, click the Send button and Outlook Express will automatically dispatch your message.

Creating new postings is one thing, but much of the time you may find yourself responding to the postings of others.

Responding is just as simple as creating messages from scratch. Simply select the message you wish to respond to and click the Reply to Group option.

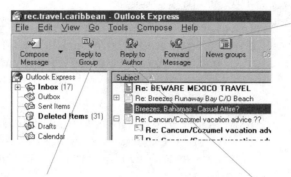

Allows a copy of the currently selected message to be sent to someone – does NOT post to the newsgroup.

Selecting this option posts a response directly into the newsgroup.

Sends a response to the message author ONLY.

Choosing to respond brings up the following dialogue box:

These are already filled in by Outlook with details from the original message.

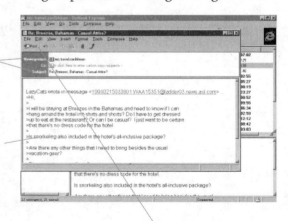

The text pane carries a copy of the original message with space at the top for you to add your own comments.

When you've finished, simply press the Post button.

Text and Binary Files

Broadly speaking there are two types of files which can be submitted to news servers: plain text files (which contain basic messages) and binary files (which are used to transmit pictures, executable files and more).

Plain text files present no problem whatsoever to Usenet news servers, which quite happily pass them around without any difficulty.

HANDY TIP

If your newsreader can't handle UUencoded files you can download a separate decoder program called Wincode from http://tucows. cableinet.co.uk/

However, executables and picture files prove to be a little more complicated as the basic Usenet service was never set up to handle anything more complicated than a maximum of several hundred lines of text and standard typewriter-style characters.

In an effort to get around this difficulty, any non-plaintext files must be especially encoded so as to be compliant with Usenet as a whole. This task is carried out by UUencoding the message.

This procedure takes a sound clip, graphic or other file and transforms it into a special code which can be safely transmitted over the Net. When it is downloaded another program, UUdecode, is used to convert it back into its original format.

Nowadays this procedure is carried out automatically by many browsers but in some cases it is necessary, or even desirable, to UUdecode a particular file outside of the news reader.

```
section 1/1   file steady.bmp   [ Wincode 2.7.3 ]

begin 644 steady.bmp
MODTJXP$`````#8$`H````6@(`,L``````J`L````!/3>`0``````
M```!````O`O;VJ`+66]O[#]`O6]8>[Q[~+y [JmV]Mo"UM·M;VU·R<G·6£SL8·
MK;6U`!~^?@"]QKT`K;6M`*FIIOUM;T·D9F6`%UM>``T;3L`K;VM`£MW=P!"
MOD(`2E]G`)REIO!GB($`:I;)`"Z!!,P!!4E<`I;VM`+W&£Q0`£&D;8`6GM5#({
M2#!2!:V,`<XR,%9;:7@"EI;4`9FG&£-K;P!@@%<`B(£5^`*VMIO!·D`+4Y;
M`)REG#!O;V`6EI2·`B1D0`'2&B`1C<T`]2<G!S55@`2U9V9V·`>4G`@@8V£8`
MODI2`$%+O@@!!LLC9O;W=C·£U£$30!#7£P·K;VU`·,OO""O;T·I;6<·#]((3`!!
M87`\*4`1E`&£-UOD#2SL8·O8Y_•"%4·Ol;C-V<·/4Bl·#<L&P!J7U@`4£Y5·£MP
MD`!F5T@·;WMK`>,D`"%&&<`B:·6`&(B<IO"OAY`4OXY`(2(D!%5*5`*E·6E
M#--1@"UO<8·5D9"·&UZDP`J1DM`+D$$·"MFF£00!!"5&@·1C<_·+7&OO!.2RT`
M;WN(`<5£Q=P!C!C94·@Q!Q#&#·&<60`3·T("76)`Q`>J!>P`6=ET"·8)S``Y·C@!"
M8H£S`>IZ9·£JM5P!!/:XL`(3·9`(F(<P·)·5(C·£)D]($Y:18`K`1H`79J!`)F;
MB0!7AI``2E=@``£E=J"<G$4 NKKJ"#!D""`Z+:E(K;%#&<`5F=<·J(WA!6=2S·CA=
M`£R70"UN<8·+F!"^`$IVC0!:VSL`2G-BH£%88@@!O;WD·E+2Q·X7H+"<K:T"
M:9;6``&G·"%G·"FI8`*JGG·*RLL2GR4`"EF·161DD'7`1,!``66UM`O"(
MI:4O<[<£$5$6'!^,8('·8RM££5F4P!`2W<·5H;L`%5`6@@(H£F£^),C5S``)N£
MD"!02P;G£VE(R01O"<K;4'9INU·+7&MO"·£Ck)'7k-8`)2MIO"(ION£·@(IK@·M;VE
M`)·9K0"UM;T`SL;£·£·6@^-@P"46GG@*4`CHZ<`*VUOO`2H£(·I+£6]·N>NO"BP+T`
MH£"F]]··2>M`"]QK4·B)BU·)RUMO"CL<4·E+£Z`,;]MO"EG"4·I924·+W!KO"4
ML;$·K;6M`-·5SP£#£QLX`D;;;·(*W&Q@(""£IL£·M<;£`;£O0O"<K9P·H+W,'£E
MKO"OM\\`O;6]·+6MOO"HHY<·M:V<·,£MO"UM:4`O<:M·*£B"MO"]<O<X£B*VE
M`,;;.U@"]M:4`O;W&£·+VUMO"]SK4`K[+6·,;£MO"MO:4`O<;6`)BOIO#&UKT`
```

UUencoded files are easy to spot. Every line begins with an M and is a fixed length string of ASCII characters.

Reading and Composing Offline

Dealing with your news traffic online can be an expensive business, especially if you subscribe to a large number of groups.

Much of the time the difficulty lies not with the actual download of the messages but with the time it takes to physically read each message and then to type appropriate replies.

A much more efficient (and cheaper!) way of reading the latest information from the groups is to do it offline, which gives you all the time in the world to prepare responses and thoroughly browse any messages which take your fancy.

Using Outlook Express, the easiest way to set up your subscribed groups for offline reading is to highlight your group of choice then select the Properties option of the File menu. When the dialogue box appears select the second tab, marked Download (see below). The options presented in this box will determine how Outlook Express deals with your newsgroup messages.

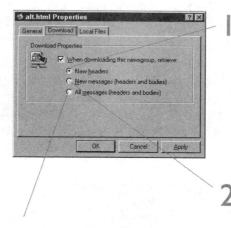

This option will download only the message headers, allowing you to select which to download in full based on the author, subject line or date.

2 This option will download all new messages which have appeared since you last checked the group.

3 Downloads everything irrespective of age (or relevance!).

Choosing to download the message headers alone is quite quick and allows individual notes to be selected for download in full.

Selecting the messages is simply a matter of following these easy steps:

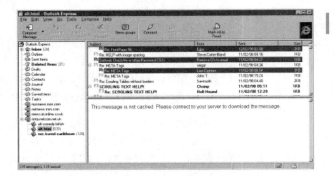

Highlight the messages you wish to download.

2 Right-click with the mouse and select Mark message for download.

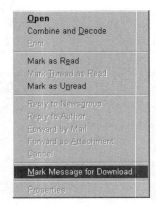

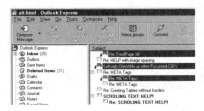

3 Outlook helpfully places a download icon to show which messages you require.

When you have finished marking off the messages for download, all of the selected entries can be retrieved by going back on-line and selecting Download this Newsgroup.

It is worth airing a note of caution at this point: it's very easy to get carried away, subscribe to dozens of newsgroups then decide to read every entry. This can amount to hundreds – even thousands – of messages every day which can be an impossible amount to cover.

What makes it even more of a task (and increases the expense dramatically) is if you subscribe to the binary newsgroups, which carry images, programs, utilities, sounds and more.

Downloading the vast quantities of data carried in such groups can take hours and potentially leave you with many megabytes of data which you don't particularly want.

The best strategy to adopt when accessing Usenet is to start small and work your way up to a comfortable level. It's far better to have subscriptions to just a handful of groups and a small phone bill than to go crazy and face the financial consequences later on.

Take care when downloading files from binary groups as it is possible some of them may contain viruses which could harm your computer. Always use a virus checker on such programs before you execute them.

Some Useful Software

If you don't fancy using Outlook Express as your primary newsreader, try some of the following packages:

FreeAgent – http://www.forteinc.com/agent
WinVn – http://www.ksc.nasa.gov/software/winvn/winvn.html
News Xpress – http://tucows.cableinet.co.uk/adnload/
dlnxpress.html

If you're looking for news items relating to a particular subject, try the Deja News search engine which can search entries from thousands of groups in just a few seconds:

http://www.dejanews.com

If DejaNews doesn't take your fancy why not try NewsFerret, a fast and highly efficient package which does an excellent job of rooting out those hard-to-find news articles.

NewsFerret can be found at:

http://www.ferretsoft.com

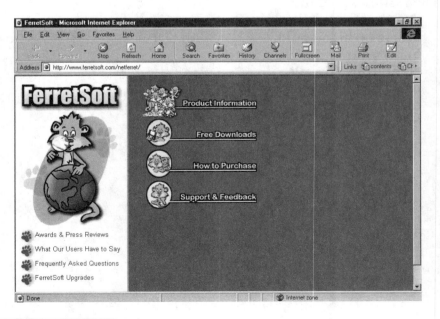

FTP

For many people the World Wide Web IS the Internet, but look a little deeper under the skin and you'll find a whole lot more, including the very useful File Transfer Protocol (FTP).

Covers

Chapter Six

What is FTP?

It is a common misconception that the World Wide Web IS the Internet. In fact, nothing could be further from the truth.

The origins of the Net date back to the early part of the 1960s when the American military created a basic networking system which could survive a potential nuclear attack.

It wasn't until nearly 30 years later that a British scientist, Tim Berners-Lee, came up with the idea for hypertext documents and the Web was born.

Prior to the advent of the Web were a range of protocols used to navigate and search the Internet with interesting and intriguing names such as Telnet, WAIS and Jughead.

Probably the most popular however was FTP or File Transfer Protocol – one of the most basic functions of the Internet and one of the most important.

Across the Net there are thousands and thousands of FTP servers dedicated to allowing users to download, and upload, data and other information.

With the explosion in popularity of the Web, the use of FTP for many people has obviously fallen dramatically but for situations where it is necessary to pass files between individuals there is still no real substitute for a good FTP client and a fast server connection!

FTP with a Browser

As technology moves on and the web gets older, enterprising developers seem intent on producing software packages that can do a little bit of everything.

Modern web browser software is capable of performing a wide range of functions that only a few years ago required a number of different packages. This includes the capability to download files via FTP over the web.

To the user the whole operation is seamless and to the person who created the web page in the first place there is little more complexity – it's just a matter of inserting a hyperlink directly to the file or document in question rather than to another HTML page.

One of the more recent additions to the browser arsenal is the ability to upload files to Internet servers as well as to download. This facility is restricted to a very small subset of the browsers around today and cannot be relied upon, so for the time being it is probably best to stick to a dedicated FTP client like CuteFTP or WS FTP.

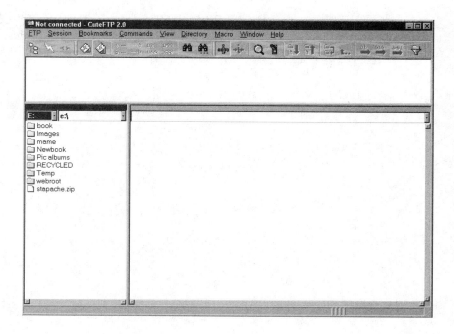

Types of FTP

Broadly speaking there are two distinct types of FTP – private and public (or anonymous, as it is commonly known).

Private FTP requires the person accessing the FTP server to have a special username and password. If you try to gain access to files on the server without these you'll simply be denied.

This kind of restricted access is used for situations such as those where private companies want to give subscribers and customers, but not the general public, access to files and documents. This usually means a systems administrator will have to maintain a special set of passwords and usernames, one for every person who wants, or needs, access.

Anonymous FTP is provided by those who don't mind who has access to the files on their server. There are many sites across the net which actively encourage public access and so have created a special anonymous account.

Anonymous access requires no special password or username, instead using anonymous as the username and your e-mail address as the password.

FTP in Action

With the explanations out of the way, it's time to get down to the serious business of looking at how to carry out FTP operations.

The first step is to get hold of a good FTP program.

HANDY TIP

CuteFTP can be downloaded from http://www.cuteftp.com

Most PC and Macintosh-based systems come equipped with a basic package as standard, but these require an understanding of how to use command line operations and are probably best left to those who prefer to use the old-fashioned DOS-style interface.

For the purposes of this chapter we'll be using the shareware CuteFTP package for the PC, but the basics of using this package apply equally to many other client programs.

On running the program, the first thing that confronts the user is the FTP Manager screen where new sites can be added to the internal bookmarks list or existing ones can be edited or deleted as appropriate.

This pane shows any folders which may have been set up to contain sites.

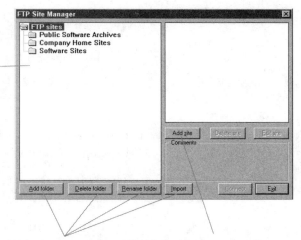

These buttons help to keep order of your favourite sites and import settings from other FTP programs.

Clicking this button allows a new site to be created within the current folder.

Setting up the details for a new FTP site is as easy as clicking the Add Site button.

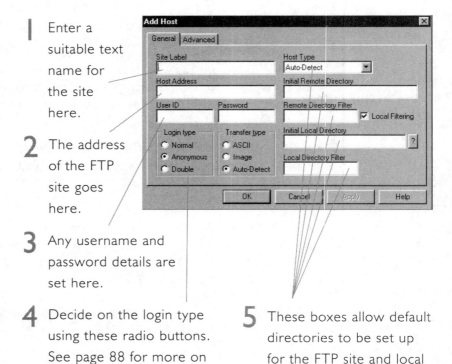

1 Enter a suitable text name for the site here.

2 The address of the FTP site goes here.

3 Any username and password details are set here.

4 Decide on the login type using these radio buttons. See page 88 for more on anonymous FTP.

5 These boxes allow default directories to be set up for the FTP site and local machine.

It is essential that the details required in steps one through four are entered in order to correctly set up a new FTP site.

The information required in step five can be regarded as 'advanced' and need only be entered if it is known.

With the details for the FTP site now set up, it's time to go on-line and explore the delights of what the server has to offer.

These buttons make using CuteFTP easy (see below for more details).

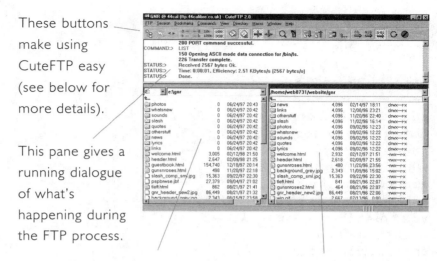

This pane gives a running dialogue of what's happening during the FTP process.

Local files (those on your machine) are shown here.

Files on the remote server are shown here,

The diagram above shows neatly what the individual elements of an FTP client do but it also points out the one big drawback of using FTP.

Take a quick look at the right-hand pane of the CuteFTP window, which shows the contents of the remote server.

It gives a functional view of all of the files which are available for download but it doesn't say what they are. For many people this can be a major disadvantage as they risk spending time downloading files they may not want.

However, if you do happen to know what the files are and what you are looking for, FTP holds many advantages over other methods of file retrieval – it's faster and more reliable for a start.

Leaving the relative pros and cons of using FTP to one side, let's move back to the icons CuteFTP presents for performing file transfer operations.

Don't worry if you can't remember all of these functions. CuteFTP provides handy tool-tips which give a brief explanation of what each icon means if you point the mouse over them for a short period of time.

Opens the site manager

Breaks the current connection

Options for sorting directory entries

Views currently selected file

Change directory up/down

Refresh file list/ stop operation

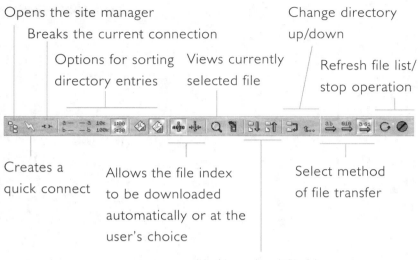

Creates a quick connect

Allows the file index to be downloaded automatically or at the user's choice

Select method of file transfer

Up/download file(s)

As you can see there a great many options available through CuteFTP to help keep control of all aspects of the file transfer procedure, which is as easy to carry out as this:

After selecting a suitable site from the site manager we've logged in using anonymous FTP. The list of files now appears.

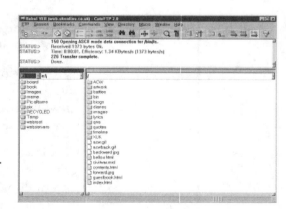

HANDY TIP

Multiple files can be selected by clicking on the first then shift-clicking on the last file you require.

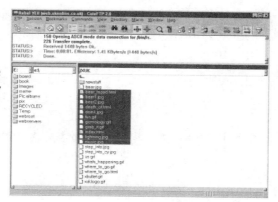

2 The files to be downloaded are selected by using standard point and click techniques.

3 We tell CuteFTP to download the files by either selecting the appropriate button from the toolbar or by dragging and dropping the selected files from right pane to left pane. This dialogue box then appears.

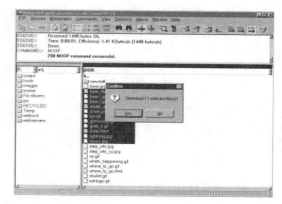

HANDY TIP

To upload files simply reverse this procedure, moving files from the left pane to the right. Remember, however, you will need permission to upload files to the vast majority of FTP servers.

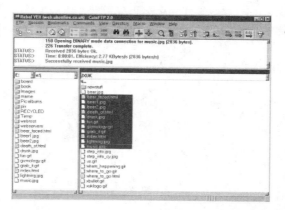

4 After a short wait the files are shown in the left pane, indicating that they have been transferred successfully.

Alternative FTP Software

There are literally dozens of high quality FTP packages around on the Internet and the "best" is really a matter of opinion.

Listed below are just a handful of programs you might like to try.

Bulletproof FTP – http://www.bpftp.com/

> A feature-packed program which will allow files from several different directories to be downloaded at the same time as well as providing a resume facility which allows "broken" download to be completed at a later date.

Cupertino – http://www.members.xoon.com/~seanhu

> A freeware package (you don't have to pay if it is intended solely for private use) which provides auto resume, a site manager and many more features.

WS-FTP – http://www.ipswitch.com/Products/WS_FTP/ index.html

> Another package which is free to non-commercial users which provides a hatful of useful functions, including the ability to modify file attributes on UNIX servers.

Netiquette

To date there are no set of hard and fast rules governing the Internet and the way it is regulated and used.

Instead, there are a number of unwritten rules which Net users are expected to adhere to, and which are drawn together under the heading of netiquette. In this chapter we'll take a look at how to do things the right way and avoid the wrath of other Net users.

Introduction

In the real world there are many ways in which we can all be good citizens: from helping old ladies across the road to keeping an eye on a neighbour's cat when she's away on holiday.

Things operate in a different way on the Internet – for a start there are very few cats on-line.

Good on-line citizens, or netizens as they are known, stick to a set of unofficial rules which have developed over the years to make the Net a good place to be. This set of rules puts tolerance and patience at its core and expects that all Net users exercise a little care and respect in all their dealings.

It's a nice idea; unfortunately it doesn't always work …

For detailed discussion on this read Internet Culture in easy steps, in this same series.

For some there are basic mistakes and errors of judgement to be made. Beginners who don't know a lot about the way the Internet works can often find themselves on the receiving end of sarcastic comments from those who have been around a little longer. For a tiny minority, however, abusing others and causing electronic mayhem becomes a way of life.

Take time to read the following pages and become familiar with some of the buzzwords and the pitfalls that new users can fall into and then avoid them! In the long term it's far better to go out onto the wild and woolly electronic frontier with a six-shooter loaded with knowledge than to get there and find you're firing blanks ….

Flaming

Flaming is an activity which is usually linked with posting into the newsgroups.

Flames are designed to provoke a reaction, stir up trouble or just to cause a rash of follow-up postings relating to some pointless, and usually off-topic, subject.

 For more information on newsgroups see chapter 5.

It's amazing how quickly an insulting message can start a flurry of responses, commonly known as a flame war (because the insults fly back and forth and everyone gets caught up in the crossfire).

There are times when you may feel that someone has done (or typed) something which is deliberately inflammatory and deserves to be admonished. Be warned! They may not have meant what they typed.

The problem with conversations and debates carried out solely using text is that it's all too easy to misconstrue what others are saying. The art of sarcasm and the use of the odd wry comment can provoke a storm of protest if someone reads what you've written but doesn't actually fully understand what it is you're really trying to say.

In order to make life easier some enterprising soul created the concept of the emoticon (or smiley as it is commonly known).

The smiley, :), is used to indicate when someone is making a funny remark. Originally there was just the one comprising a colon followed by a right-hand bracket. Over time the number of smileys has ballooned and there are now hilarious smiling faces for just about any occasion you can think of.

A liberal use of these grinning icons can help to diffuse statements which could potentially cause offence to others so feel free to use them whenever the situation warrants it. If you choose not to do so, be sure to read all of your outgoing messages before hitting the Send button, or face the potential consequences :)

Some of the more common smileys include:

:-)	basic smiley
;-)	cheeky grin
:-(	upset
:-C	terribly upset
:->	devilish grin
B-)	wearing spectacles
:-O	amazed
B:-)	glasses on head
{:-)	toupee wearer
}:-)	toupee wearer in strong wind
:-[	vampire
:^)	big nose
:-9	yum!
%-|	been staring at the screen too long
:-P	grinning from side of mouth
:-|	not terribly amused
8-|	eyes wide in surprise
8-O	ohmigod!
:-D	big grin!
:-&	tongue-tied
:-X	lips are sealed

And for the really outrageous ...

=|:-)=	typist is Abraham Lincoln

HANDY TIP

For a more complete smiley list, visit http://paul.merton.ox.ac.uk/ascii/smiley.html

Spamming

Spamming is a major issue on the Internet at the current time. A spam is an e-mail message which is sent to hundreds (or even thousands, or tens of thousands of people) at random or is posted to many, many newsgroups at the same time.

HANDY TIP

For more on spamming, pop over to http:// www.bitgate.com/ spam/

Usually spam messages bear no relevance to the groups in which they are posted or have no particular relevance to the individuals who receive them – they are the electronic equivalent of junk mail.

Generally speaking spam can be split into two groups: the "Get rich quick" schemes and the "appeal" messages.

"Get rich quick" messages invariably centre around some form of money making racket which claims you will make thousands of dollars (or pounds) within a short space of time. Not only are they annoying when they drop into your electronic mail box, but they are also (usually) a con.

The second category of spam doesn't make anyone any money but can cause great inconvenience. This usually revolves around a child with a serious illness who is trying to get into the Guinness Book of World Records by collecting the world's greatest number of postcards/ beermats/business cards (etc).

Spammers often go to great lengths to disguise their true e-mail identities in order to fend off furious replies from hundreds of disgruntled net users who are upset at unsolicited mail.

In many cases, those reported of having sent spam mail can expect to have their accounts cancelled by their ISP.

In several recent test cases spammers have been fined thousands of pounds by ISPs for misuse of computer equipment, and under laws currently being considered in some countries may even face jail sentences.

If all of this sounds a little scary, don't let it put you off; just take care with your postings.

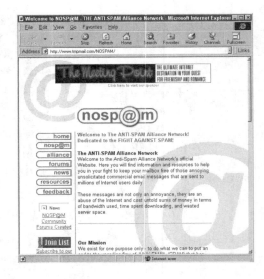

Messages relating to commercial products should only be posted into relevant newsgroups and cross-posted messages should be targeted carefully. There's no point in sending info on cat food to a group discussing aerodynamics for example.

For a more detailed look at spam why not visit some of these informative sites:

Anti-Spam Alliance Network
    http://www.delphi.com/NOSPAM/

The MMF Hall of Humiliation
    http://ga.to/mmf/
    A site which looks at the best, the worst and most outrageous "Get Rich Quick" messages of the week

Erinn's Anti-Spam page
    http://www.flinet.com/~erwyn/spam/

Get That Spammer!
    http://kryten.eng.monash.edu.au/gspam.html

General Rules

There are many ways to fall foul of the unwritten rules of the Internet, but if you take heed of the tips that follow you should have a reasonable chance of avoiding the more common problems.

1   Don't swear. OK, so it's obvious really, but you would be amazed at the number of people who land themselves in trouble by being foul-mouthed.

2   When first entering a newsgroup or IRC channel, spend a little time getting a feel for the type and style of conversation. This will allow you to chat with confidence.

3   Always read the FAQ (Frequently Asked Questions) list for a channel or group if one exists. FAQs will answer all of the simple queries newbies have and will help you to avoid look foolish by speaking out too soon!

4   DON'T TYPE EVERYTHING IN CAPITALS!!!!! Capitals are the Net equivalent of shouting and no-one likes a shouter ...

5   Think before you type. Remember that it's easy for innocent phrases to be misinterpreted by others. Gratuitous use of smileys will help avoid disaster.

6   Be courteous. Please and Thank You go a long way, especially if you need a lot of help over a period of time.

7   Starting a deliberate war of words over IRC is not big and not clever. You could find yourself barred from particular channels or servers if you try to put someone down in the wrong way or in the wrong area.

8   As mentioned earlier this chapter, don't spam! If you must cross-post to several newsgroups make sure what you have to say is relevant. The penalties for spamming range from a mailbox full of irate e-mails from spam victims to the suspension of your Net account and potentially even legal action.

9   If you're replying to a newsgroup posting, only quote as much of the original message as you need to. There's nothing worse when browsing the groups than to find a 60 line note to which someone has added the phrase "I agree."

10 Stick to the point! There is nothing more infuriating then reading through the contents of rec.pets.cats and finding a posting from someone who wants to sell his lawnmower.

Security & Social Issues

There are many new and interesting ways in which it is possible to fall foul of the law on the Internet.

This chapter takes a look at the legal and social problems of the electronic frontier.

Chapter Eight

Covers

Computer Viruses

There can be no excuse for the writing of viruses and there's certainly nothing worse than finding out your PC is infected with one.

A virus is a malicious computer program which can do a variety of potentially disastrous things. Like infections in human beings, computer viruses spread through contact; in the case of the PC, by putting the source of the infection (usually a floppy disk or downloaded program) onto your PC and then running it.

HANDY TIP

Protect yourself from infection by getting hold of a good virus checker – visit http://www. mcafee.com or http:// www.symantec.com

The malicious code may sit around doing nothing for days, weeks or even months before it triggers itself and the results may range from simply playing an annoying and pointless tune to the destruction of data on hard disks.

It is difficult to say why anyone would want to write such a program in the first place. Rarely is it done for financial gain and viruses are more of a nuisance than anything else.

The best way to protect yourself is to get hold of a good quality anti-virus package for your computer, from a firm such as Norton Computing or McAfee which can be updated on a monthly basis with all of the latest information on problem files.

The only way to ensure you never catch a virus is not to download a file onto your computer from the Internet. This of course defeats much of the point in having such a huge information archive at your fingertips, so a virus checker is really an essential tool to have installed on your computer.

It goes without saying, of course, that deliberately passing files to friends and colleagues which are infected is a very silly thing to do. Far from being a joke it can result in a lot of destruction and leave the "victim" of your fun having to spend a lot of time picking up the pieces...

Hacking

In the early days of computing and the Internet, hackers were the elite group of computer programmers who produced the software that made things happen. Hackers were most often found on University campuses fixing bugs in existing system software or creating new programs that did things no-one had thought possible. As the years passed, however, the definition became twisted from it's roots and the word hacker was associated with the computer underground and with those who made it their aim to beat the security systems surrounding existing Internet systems.

Some hackers were content to "hack" their way past said security then brag about it to their friends. Others went one step further and stole information which was commercially and/or militarily sensitive.

Many hackers, such as American super hacker Kevin Mitnick, have gone down in computer history for their exploits but it's only fair to point out that they "went down" in more ways than one – the strong arm of the law does not appreciate illegal attempts to pry into the secrets of others.

There's one only one rule when it comes to the subject of hacking – DON'T DO IT! There are hundreds, if not thousands, of web pages across the Net dedicated to the study and pursuit of hacking. Some even contain program segments which will allow anyone who downloads them to perform certain "operations" on the systems of others. But remember: whilst it is not always illegal to download such software you may well face serious trouble if you try them out. You have been warned ...

For an excellent look at what happened during a major anti-hacker investigation read Bruce Sterling's "The Hacker Crackdown" at http://www. softlab.ntua.gr/ internet/crackdown/ crack_toc.html

Pirate Software

Pirate software is illegal. End of story.

The electronic community is no different from any other; it has it's fair share of wheeler-dealers, wide-boys and out-and-out villains.

The Software Publishers Association have a wonderfully informative website at http://www.spa. org/piracy/q&a.htm

As you may expect there are a lot of sites around which deal with pirated (illegally copied) games and application software, offering programs worth hundreds and even thousands of pounds to anyone who wants them for the cost of a download from the Internet.

Throughout the computing industry piracy has become a real problem, costing software companies a phenomenal amount of money in lost sales each year.

As well as the criminal side of piracy (you could be sent to jail for possession of pirate software) it's also worth bearing in mind that there is a moral side too, If piracy continues to increase, sales revenue for the software companies will fall, making it less attractive for them to release new and updated packages and let's face it, what would the world be without Quake II or Microsoft Word?

Pornography

Yes, it's true, there is porn on the Internet.

It's also true to say that there is a great deal of porn around in the "real world" – if you're prepared to look for it.

Recent media attention would have you believe there are naked, writhing bodies around every corner of every webpage but the truth isn't quite that bad!

HANDY TIP

If you have kids, or just don't fancy the thought of stumbling across net porn try auto-censoring like NetNanny (http://www.netnanny.com) or CyberSitter (http://www.cybersitter.com)

Like the other subjects covered in this chapter it's a fact of life and everyone who uses the Net should be aware that it exists.

Given the lack of any concrete laws regarding the spread of pornographic material on the net, and the fact that what may be considered unacceptable in one country may be looked upon more 'liberally' elsewhere – which is just a mouseclick away for the casual net user – it has proved almost impossible to police such information. Indeed, in the USA in late 1997, attempts to pass the Communications Decency Act were thwarted when the courts ruled that the terms of the legal bill were too restrictive on the rights of the American people to free speech.

For adults it is simply a matter of choice – whether to look at a particular website which contains pornographic material, or not.

The problem for many people comes when youngsters have access to it.

To help alleviate some of the problems caused by this moral dilemma there are a number of software solutions which can be used by parents to stop their offspring from viewing material deemed to be unsuitable.

Such censorship (or screening) software may use a variety of approaches to block content: from fuzzing out parts of pictures – in much the same way as police programmes on TV sometimes mask the faces of people who are arrested – to scanning the text of a page to check for the presence of certain specified words.

Even the humble web browser goes some way to helping in the fight against unsuitable content.

From release 3, Internet Explorer allowed content to be effectively barred to the viewer by embracing the RSACI (Recreational Software Advisory Council on the Internet) standards. Under these rules sexual content, bad language, adult themes and more are rated by the site creator on a sliding scale. The PC owner at home can set a maximum suitable level for each of the categories and anything above that level will be blocked by the browser.

For more information on the RSACI visit http:// www.rsac.org/ homepage.asp

In essence it's a great idea, but the problem is that the entire scheme relies on the site maintainer 'grading' his or her own content. Obviously, there is plenty of opportunity for mistakes to be made and deliberate mis-gradings to be given, so bear this in mind in you follow the rules and regulations of the organisation!

At the end of the day there is little that is going to stop a determined teenager from getting hold of one porn picture or another and probably the best way of ensuring youngsters use the Net to best effect is to surf along with them.

The advantages of this approach are many: it allows the kids to make the best of a wonderful information resource, it allows parents to get some value from the very expensive computer equipment they bought for the family and it makes learning a valuable family experience.

Legal Issues

All of the subjects examined in this chapter are illegal in one way or another and should be treated with the utmost seriousness.

Because of the lack of laws and any formal police force the Internet has been dubbed by some as the New Wild West.

The problem currently is that different countries are passing laws and making rules and regulations over web content which others have yet to get around to.

This means that what is OK in say, the Netherlands, may be totally illegal in the UK. Some argue that if this is the case then it's simply a matter of moving sensitive content to rented webspace in another country, but this is not necessarily so.

The web is growing at an astonishing rate and as it explodes in popularity more and more laws are being passed and more people are becoming aware of the ways in which the Net can be exploited.

At this juncture it would be impossible to say exactly what is and what isn't illegal. The safest way to stay on the right side of the law is to abide by the laws governing ways and means in other walks of life – or get a really good lawyer.

A Final Word

If what you have read in this chapter has convinced you that the entire Internet is nothing more than a depraved den of inequity populated by perverts and scavengers then you couldn't be more wrong!

It's true that the Net does have its fair share of dark and dingy corners, but thankfully it's usually pretty difficult to walk into them and it's very easy to walk away.

As issues regarding the legality of content on the Net draw more and more attention from the general public, more and more illegal sites are disappearing. Those which stretch the bounds of legality (and in some cases decency) are installing disclaimer pages which warn of what lies behind them.

The only way to make sure the content is fit for you and your children is to exercise a little caution when approaching information which may not be 100% suitable.

Although the Internet has been viewed as the new TV there is still a radical difference between the standards imposed by the BBC and ITV, with their watersheds and strict rules, and the relative anarchy of the Internet.

Internet Chat

E-mail and newsgroups aren't the only ways to communicate with others using the Internet.

For those who really love to chat in real time there's always the option of IRC (Internet Relay Chat).

Covers

Chapter Nine

Introduction

Whilst e-mail is a wonderful invention that allows people from all over the world to communicate with one another, it's still a little bit slow for some.

The hours it can take for a message to blaze a trail half way around the world before picking up a reply can all get a bit too much for some people.

However, help is at hand, not only for the impatient but for those who love to have a good chat, in the form of IRC (Internet Relay Chat).

Whilst e-mail is the online equivalent of Her Majesty's Post Office, IRC is most definitely the CB radio of the Internet and is used by tens of thousands of people every day to natter away on every topic known to man (and woman of course).

IRC is a very immediate communication method. It relies on a set of special servers linked right across the globe which pass messages to others within seconds and can bring them back to the sender in the same amount of time.

It's a bit like an ordinary phone call, with the exception that the whole conversation is carried out in a text only format (see Chapter 11 for information on net telephony and video conferencing) but this doesn't deter people from joining in more than 13,000 different topics of conversation (and that's in the UK and Europe alone!).

Chat Clients

There are a variety of software packages that can be used to access the IRC networks, each with their own strengths and weaknesses.

It's entirely possible to connect up using a program called Telnet, which has been around since the very early days of the Net, but this tends to be a very complicated and involved process which is more suited to the seasoned user – and as any seasoned user will tell you, there's no substitute for a proper client package!

For the PC, probably the best known and most widely used package is a shareware program called mIRC which surprisingly (for the Internet anyway) is a British package written by an enterprising gentleman called Khaled Mardam-Bey.

Over the last couple of years, mIRC has developed into a package to be reckoned with and contains just about every feature you could ever hope to see in an IRC client, giving complete control over the way the user sees and accesses the IRC networks.

 For more information on mIRC visit http:// www.mirc.co.uk

However, mIRC isn't the only package available, and a trip to one of the bigger shareware archives will yield many different programs to try out until a suitable one is discovered.

For a comprehensive list of the freeware and shareware IRC clients visit:

http://www.winfiles.com – The Windows 95/98 shareware archive

http://tucows.cableinet.co.uk – The Ultimate Collection of Winsock Software

Setting Up

For the purposes of the rest of this chapter we'll be using the mIRC program to demonstrate how to get online and start chatting but, as ever, the instructions given here are equally as applicable to most other packages.

1 Download the program from the Net and install it to your hard drive.

2 Run the program.

3 mIRC will open up and present the dialogue box below.

This window and buttonset allow the user to set up a list of preferred IRC servers

Follow steps 4,5,6 & 7 for instructions on what to do with these

You must supply mIRC with a nickname – this is the name you will be identified by when you connect to IRC.

HANDY TIP

Filling in these boxes gives details which will help identify you to others

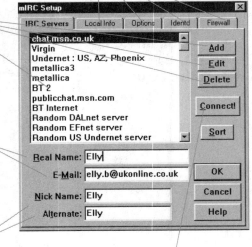

Nicknames are essential when using IRC. They can be funny, imaginative or you can use your own name

Clicking here will connect you to a chosen server

4 Do as the instructions tell you on this tab; mIRC will automatically determine what needs to go here.

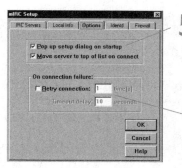

5 Selecting this option will ensure the dialog box from step 1 appears every time mIRC is started.

Setting these details specifies how many times the program will attempt to connect to an IRC server.

6 As with step 4 it is probably best to leave this alone unless you're a bit of an expert.

7 This option allows you to use mIRC from behind a firewall. If you don't know what a firewall is you probably don't need to fill in these details.

Connecting to a Server

With the software set up it's time to venture out into the wide world of IRC.

The first thing that's required is a suitable server to connect to. This is essential as messages typed by you will be sent directly to the server which will then pass that message to dozens of other servers across the IRC network. In turn those servers will pass the message along again until it has been propagated across participating computers.

There is a huge list of IRC servers to be found at http:// www.astraweb.com/ jayr/

As you may have guessed, with many thousands of people using the system at any one time there are an incredible number of messages flying around. Thanks to the fact that these messages are mainly text based this is a very quick operation and someone in Jamaica, Russia or Australia will see what you have typed within a matter of seconds of hitting the Return key on your keyboard.

Many ISPs have their own IRC servers these days so it's best to check with your service provider so see if they have this facility for you to use. If not, you'll have to take pot luck and try one of the public access machines which are provided by a small group of kindly souls.

Unfortunately, because of the huge popularity of the service and the demands placed on the computer hardware which runs it, the number of freely accessible IRC servers is slowly dwindling and gaining access to one can be quite tricky.

Presuming you're using one of the more established providers let's crack on and take a quick peek at how the process works:

Starting mIRC brings up the standard dialogue box.

...cont'd

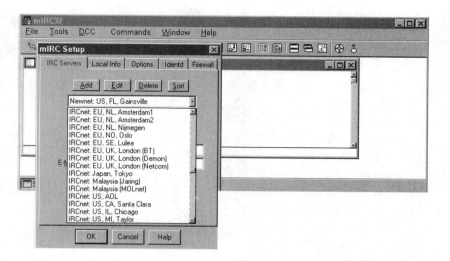

2 Clicking in the drop-down box reveals a list of IRC servers. If new ones become available use the buttons to add their details. Just select a suitable local server and hit the OK button.

#newbies is a good channel to head for if you are a beginner.

3 After a few seconds mIRC will connect you to the server, which responds with a Welcome message, giving the latest information on the state of the network.

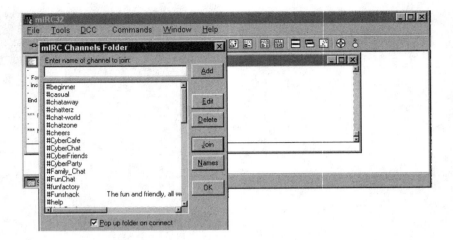

4   Being a thorough package, mIRC even gives you a dialogue
    box filled with some of the more popular chat channels on
    the network. If none of the offered choices sound
    interesting, a personal choice can be entered into the area
    at the top.

5   After choosing a channel it's time to enter the world of on-
    line chat – have fun!

Channel Listings

Once you've made it online it can be a tricky business deciding what to do next.

The key to navigating a route through the IRC jungle is getting to grips with the channels.

Each channel on the IRC network is a separate chat room dedicated to a particular subject – for example, entering a channel named #pigeons would normally place you squarely in the centre of cut and thrust debate relating to our feathered friends.

In the real virtual world things may turn out to be quite different and #pigeons may be filled with scintillating chatter about the weather – ah well, life, eh?

BEWARE

Given the popularity of IRC getting a listing of all of the available channels can take quite a long time!

Should you fancy surfing around the world of IRC the best place to start is with the full list of existing channels.

Just type /list (include the forward slash too) and within a few moments a new window containing information on all the channels will appear:

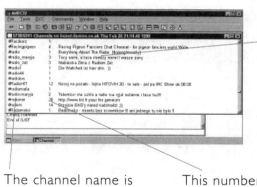

A short description of what the channel is all about (sometimes the descriptions don't make much sense!)

The channel name is given here

This number relates to the number of people chatting in each channel

Joining a Channel

Now that you know how to discover which channels are available, it's helpful to know how to join in.

Simple! Just type /join (don't forget the forward slash) followed by the channel (not forgetting the hash symbol).

So, to join a channel devoted to the computer game Quake II it is necessary to type /join #quake2 in the status window.

As soon as you hit the return key a new window will open which shows the ongoing chat in the channel you've chosen, together with some other details (see the diagram below).

HANDY TIP

Take care not to join too many channels at once or you'll lose track of the conversations!

The great thing about IRC is that you can carry out multiple conversations all at the same time. Indeed, it is possible to open many different windows, each dedicated to a separate topic. Be warned however, that while a couple of open channels can keep you busy, too many will lead to frantic periods of typing and extends sessions of scrolling backwards through windows to see what you've missed – you have been warned!

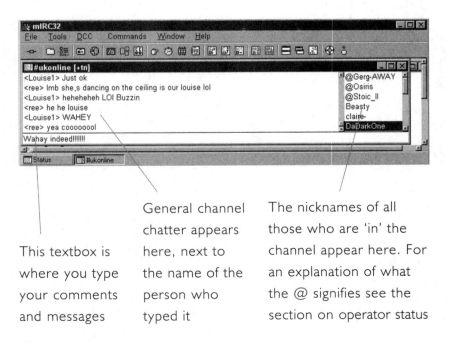

This textbox is where you type your comments and messages

General channel chatter appears here, next to the name of the person who typed it

The nicknames of all those who are 'in' the channel appear here. For an explanation of what the @ signifies see the section on operator status

Your First Chat

Making your opening gambit can seem quite daunting –
after all no-one wants to make a fool of themselves first
time out.

Here are some useful hints you might like to bear in mind
when taking the plunge for the first time:

1   Take the time to 'lurk' in the channel and get a feel for
    what others are talking about and the way in which they say
    it. It's no good launching into a spirited monologue on how
    Capt. Picard could beat Capt. Kirk in a pub fight if you're in
    a channel discussing the life and times of William
    Shakespeare!

2   Be courteous! The easiest way to make yourself unpopular
    is by being rude to other chat users.

3   Try to choose a channel that's not too busy for your first
    couple of excursions. Busy channels can be very confusing
    for the beginner as events tend to happen too quickly to
    allow a suitable period for response.

4   Don't be afraid to visit channels like #ircbar, #newbies and
    #irchelp; there are plenty of people around who will take
    time out to help you. In the finest spirit of the net, try to
    return the favour to other newbies when you have a little
    confidence in your own abilities.

If you bear in mind the above points your early experiments
should be painless and a thoroughly enjoyable experience.

There is one other point to bear in mind however, and that's the special language of IRC. Like anything with its roots in "net geekdom" IRC thrives on its specialist terms and such specialist terms, being American in nature, revolve around TLAs, or Three Letter Acronyms. Some of these acronyms have more than three letters, but hey, who's counting?

Some of the more common TLAs include:

LOL	–	Laugh Out Loud
ROFL	–	Rolls On Floor Laughing
ROFLMAO	–	Rolls On Floor Laughing My Ass Off
FYI	–	For Your Information
IMHO	–	In My Honest Opinion
FWIW	–	For What It's Worth
IYSWIM	–	If You See What I Mean
BRB	–	Be Right Back
BBL	–	Be Back Later
RTFM	–	Read The (insert expletive) Manual

IRC Commands

There's a good deal more to IRC than just plain chatting. With a little practice a great deal of control can be exercised over the way in which the chat proceeds.

As has already been seen, it is possible to issue a command directly to the IRC server by typing it straight into the chat textbox.

Each special instruction starts with a "/" so the server knows it is to execute what follows rather than just sending it out as your comments.

Commands can perform a wide range of actions. Some of the more useful ones include:

/join #<channel> – allows you to join the specified channel (eg. /join #pigeons).

/part #<channel> – leave a channel.

/me <message> – allows you to "describe" an action (eg. /me receives the cheque and jumps for joy!).

/msg <nickname> <message> – allows a private message to be sent to the person using the nickname <nickname> (eg. / msg Snakey This is a private message, no-one else can see it).

/whois <nickname> – displays the details of the person called <nickname> (eg. /whois ragman).

/quit <message> – disconnects you from the IRC server but leaves a short message before doing so (eg. /quit It's teatime, bbl!).

/away <message> – tells people you are temporarily away from the keyboard (eg. /away Gone to fridge to get lager).

/list – lists all available channels. For a more selective list try /list -min5 -max15 (finds all channels with between 5 and 15 users) or /list *games* (finds all channels with the word games in them).

HANDY TIP

Don't forget that help is always at hand. Most good IRC clients list all of the more common commands in help files.

Private Chats

IRC is a great place to pitch into a conversation with dozens of others. Sometimes though, it's nice to restrict the scope of the conversation to one-on-one.

The easiest way to carry out a private conversation is through the use of the /msg command. Every time you wish to send a private message just type /msg <nickname of person to send to> <message>.

Take care when conducting chats in private and public at the same time. It's all too easy to get the chat windows mixed up and say something personal to anyone who is looking!

For the odd remark or comment this method is perfectly satisfactory but for longer conversations it can be a bit unwieldy so it's better to use a /query.

Typing /query <nickname of person to send to> <message> will send the appropriate message to the other party, and at the same time open a window for further query messages. It's neat, quick and easy to do.

Probably the best and fastest method is to use a DCC or direct client-to-client connection in the form /dcc chat <nickname>. DCC opens a direct line of communication between you and the other chatter which absolutely no-one else can see.

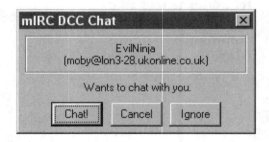

After you've typed the DCC command the intended recipient will see a dialogue box pop up on-screen asking if they wish to accept the DCC connection. All that's required is for them to hit the Accept, or Chat button and the fun can begin! If you don't feel like a private chat just hit the Cancel button – they can always try to start the chat again at a later stage. Finally, using the Ignore button will stop further chat requests from the person currently trying to chat with you – this can be really useful if someone is pestering you and you don't want to listen to them.

Starting your own Channel

So you've experimented with chatting in channels run by other people and you've built up a circle of friends through private chat: what's next?

Well, maybe it's time to create your own channel and stamp your own mark on a quiet little off-ramp of the Information Superhighway.

Creating a new channel is no more complicated than issuing any other command to the IRC server – indeed, it's made easier by the fact that there is no create channel command!

In order to start your own channel just type /join #<channelname> and you're off. The software on the IRC is bright enough to know that if you try to join a channel which doesn't exist it must create a whole new one and then inform the rest of the network that the new channel exists.

However, the creation of the channel is only one aspect of the operation as you'll need to find people to chat with – notice that when you first enter your brand-spanking-new chat area you're the only one there...

One other aspect of having your own channel, or being given a position of responsibility by another channel creator is that occasionally you will be called upon to carry out duties including dealing with troublesome users and preventing petty squabbles between users (see the next page for a look at Channel Operator status).

Operator Status

There are two kinds of people on IRC – those who are channel operators and those who aren't.

A channel operator (or chanop) is no different from anyone else on the IRC network, with the exception that they have access to a number of commands which are restricted to the rest of us.

These extra commands are usually only applicable to the channel in which the chanop has chanop status, and allow her or him to kick out and even impose a total ban on any individual, change the topic of the channel and even give chanop status to other users of the channel.

Listening to some of the conversations relating to operator status which go across IRC you may be forgiven for thinking that such an honour is only bestowed on net "experts" and long-term users of the service. This is simply not true. The easiest way to make yourself a chanop is to start your own channel. Doing so gives the first person into the channel (ie. you) automatic operator rights.

 HANDY TIP

For all the lowdown on IRC, its commands and how to deal with it, visit: http:// www.newircusers.com

So what do these extras do and how do they work? Read on to discover what power you can wield ...

/mode +o #<channame> <nickname> – this allows you to give the person using <nickname> operator status (replacing +o with -o takes the operator status away).

/mode +b #<channame> <nickname> – bans the named person from the named channel.

/mode +p <channame> – makes the channel private.

/mode +i <channame> – the channel is invite only; new users may only join if you invite them with /invite <nickname> <channame>.

/mode +l<number> <channame> – limits the number of participants to the number stated.

Scripts and Bots

IRC is no different to any other area of the Internet when it comes to complicated TLAs (see earlier this chapter for more details), plug-ins and add-on software.

Two of the biggest areas of interest outside of simple chatting concern the use of scripts and bots.

Scripts are specially written programs designed to carry out a variety of tasks – from automatically logging you onto the IRC network and auto-joining your favourite channels to generating a welcome message every time someone you know arrives on-line.

 Many IRC server owners frown on people who run bots - take care, you may be barred if your bots cause trouble.

There are a variety of these scripts around today, designed to work either from the server or to be launched through a suitable IRC client (like mIRC for example). Running scripts server-side is usually only possible if you happen to be involved in running the server. More common is client-side scripting.

Bots are a slightly different kettle of fish. Again they can be run from either the server or client-side of the equation and again the chances of running your bot server-side are about nil (unless you know the system administrator).

Bots are usually put into place to fend off the unwanted attentions of potentially malicious IRC hackers. This relatively small group of people seem to derive an odd form of pleasure from causing trouble by intruding into normally peaceful channels and attempting to take-over.

A successful take-over usually results in the gleeful hacker barring everyone from accessing the channel for a period of time – most annoying. Thankfully, bots can be launched from a chanop's client which are bright enough to detect when a potential hacker is around and fend them off.

Some Useful Software

For a broader view of IRC clients, follow these links to some excellent PC-based IRC clients.

http://tucos.cableinet.co.uk/adnload/dlorbit.html – OrbitIRC

http://www.pirchat.com – Pirch

http://www.megalith.co.uk/virc/ – VIRC 97

http://www.xircon.com/ – XIRCON

http://www.microsoft.com/ie/comichat/default.htm – MC Comic Chat

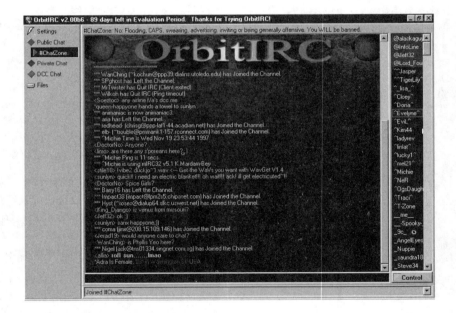

Finding the Good Stuff

In Chapter Eight we looked at some topics which give cause for concern. Now it's time to look at ways in which the Internet can yield worthwhile content.

Covers

Using Search Engines

The World Wide Web is an incredibly big place. Since its inception in the late 1980s, the ability to electronically publish material with ease has captured the imagination of Net users around the globe.

This popularity has a downside to the average surfer and for the most part that disadvantage is that finding anything can be a very tricky task.

HANDY TIP

Although most operate in a similar way, some search engines like their queries to be formatted that little bit differently. If in doubt, always check the help pages to see how to get the best from an engine.

In order to make things easier for all concerned, some enterprising souls banded together to create search engines – the Internet equivalent of a huge index, covering millions of pages and search terms.

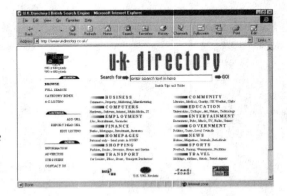

Today there are many search engines dotted around the Net, varying in quality from general content sites to highly specialised sites which focus on particular topics – healthcare, for example.

Using search engines is quite a simple operation. Just type in the words you wish to search for, press the Enter key and wait for a few seconds until the engine searches through its database and returns the relevant results.

The list of matching results can sometimes be quite long and browsing through it can be a time consuming task, so it's handy to be aware that there are a number of ways in which the search can be refined.

Search Engines – An Example

Search engines are not always the easiest of web gadgets to use so if you can find a little help to make the job easier, take it.

In the following examples we'll use Excite UK, with its wealth of features and handy options, to demonstrate how to make finding things a little simpler.

Search queries are entered here

Click here when you've finished

Allows the search to be restricted to certain areas

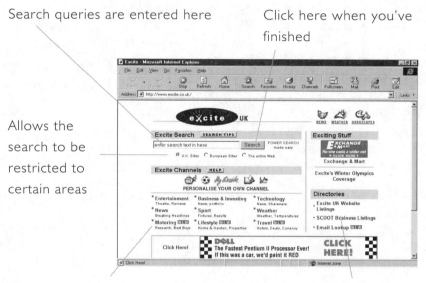

If you use search engines a lot, don't forget to add your favourites to your browser bookmarks list.

This added extra lists pre-defined top sites in a number of different areas

Some useful site directories here

A basic search can be carried out by simply entering a list of words you're looking for into the search query box and then clicking the Search button.

This kind of thing isn't always helpful however. Sometimes it's desirable to advance the type of search, to insist on the inclusion of some words and the exclusion of others.

Suppose we wanted to find information relating to the rules and regulations of the time honoured game of billiards. In the first instance we could enter a search query thus:

> billiards rules

For an in depth look at how Excite works visit the site at http://www. excite.co.uk

Whilst this is a good start there are a number of problems surrounding the way in which the query is presented. As a result of the way the engine examines the search string it will take each word as a separate entity and search for all pages which contain any, or all, of the specified words.

A quick glance through the words we've specified should be enough to see that the number of pages bearing words like billiards and rules will be huge, and not at all relevant to what we're after.

What we'd really like to see is a list of pages containing both billiards and rules (some of the pages found may still not be relevant to what we're looking for, but it's a good bet they will be in this instance).

In order to do this it is necessary to tell the search engine that the words **must** be present, a task which is carried out using the plus (+) symbol thus:

> +billiards +rules

Just as the plus forces the search to find the words billiards and rules the minus symbol (-) forces the search to exclude certain words, thus:

> +billiards +rules -american

will carry out the original search with the added advantage that it will filter out any pages which contain the word American – handy if you happen to be looking for information on the British or European game.

Boolean operations are also catered for through the use of the special phrases AND, OR, AND NOT and ().

For instance we might want to search for a page about:

> snooker AND steve AND davis

Alternatively, if Mr Davis is not the centre of attention try:

> snooker AND NOT (steve AND davis)

Finally, it's possible to enter phrases rather than individual words by surrounding the words with quotation marks.

This way, we could re-write the above query thus:

> snooker AND NOT "steve davis"

Setting the search requirement is only half of the battle however, as once the search is complete it's necessary to wade through the results:

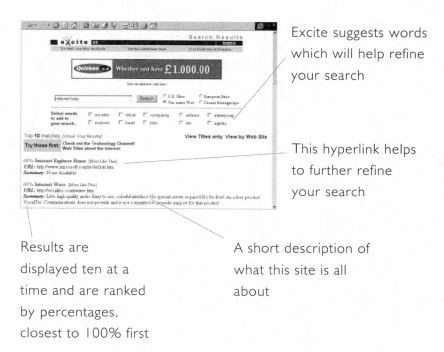

Excite suggests words which will help refine your search

This hyperlink helps to further refine your search

Results are displayed ten at a time and are ranked by percentages, closest to 100% first

A short description of what this site is all about

Search Engine Sites

Now that we've taken a look at how to search the Net, it's time to take a quick peek at a few of the more popular sites across the Net:

Yahoo!

http://www.
yahoo.co.uk

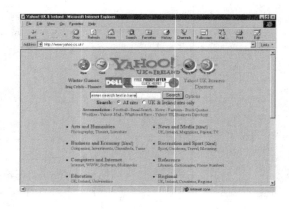

The grandfather of the Internet search engine, Yahoo! not only offers the standard search facilities but also categorises all of its entries by group and sub-group. The advantage of this approach is that it's possible to head in the right direction from the start, even before you enter search details.

Altavista

http://www.
altavista.com

An American-based engine created by computing giants Digital. Altavista is simple to use and quick to return its results, although it doesn't have many of the features of engines such as Excite.

UK Directory

http://www.ukdirectory.co.uk

Because of the way the individual search engines have been created they won't always return the same results. Enter your query into a couple of different ones to help find the matches you are looking for.

A great way to find sites based in and around the UK. The UK Directory is heavily biased towards British sites and adopts a categorised approach similar to Yahoo! to make searching easier and browsing quicker.

Yell

http://www.yell.co.uk

If at first you don't succeed, don't give up. Just structure your query in a slightly different way.

The Yellow Pages on-line provides another unique view of the electronic UK, categorised listings, a top ten of the week, and annual awards for the best home-spun sites make Yell a force to be reckoned with when it comes to finding the best of the virtual UK.

Free Software

In business there's an unwritten rule which says that there's no such thing as a free lunch, and the same holds true for the Internet – almost.

The software industry has always been a tricky beast, charging sums for its wares that range from a few pounds to figures which would make your eyes water. For the most part, the industry uses the Net as an advertising medium, offering attractive screenshots of new products and, if you're lucky, the occasional downloadable demo.

There is, however, another side to software on the Net that's much cheaper than the traditional software companies, and it wears two hats – shareware and freeware.

Shareware authors depend on your honesty when they release their treasure onto the Net. If a program's worth using it's worth paying for and payment ensures the programmer behind your favourite package will invest time in regular updates!

Freeware, as a title, says it all. It is usually written by enthusiastic amateurs and it's free to use, the cost incurred being that to download it. Why do they do it? Why not! Even in the heavily materialistic world of the 1990s there are still some people out there who produce programs just for the fun of it.

On a slightly more businesslike level comes shareware. The usual plan of action for shareware runs like this:

* Download the software from a suitable Internet site

* Try it for an initial period of, say, 30, 60 or 90 days

* When the evaluation period has expired the software will either stop functioning, disable some functions or constantly pester you with a series of advertisements or warnings until you delete it or send the author some cash

In the majority of cases there is usually an incentive to send cash; whether it's a full copy of the software on CD, printed manuals or even technical support should things go wrong.

All in all, shareware is a great way to do business for both the clients, who get to try before they buy, and the author (just ask the man behind the Paint Shop Pro art package!).

Winfiles

http://www.
winfiles.com

Sites like Winfiles will actually allow you to register some shareware software.

If it's on, it's in as the saying goes. Winfiles (formerly Windows95.com) has established itself as one of the premium Internet sites for the world's most popular operating systems.

From screensavers to screen capture programs, hardware updates to software patches, there's something for everyone here, and the enterprising folk behind the site will even sell you a multiple CD set containing thousands of shareware programs if you send them a meagre sum.

Tucows

http://tucows.
cableinet.co.uk

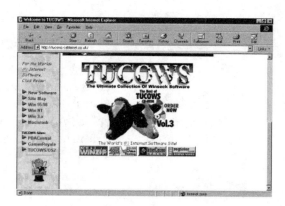

Operating in a similar vein to Windows95.com, Tucows (The Ultimate Collection of Winsock Software) concentrates its efforts on the Net market with a truly huge collection of bits and pieces for the software hungry among you. Tucows runs its only regular newsletter detailing new additions to the site and highlighting some of the better entries. It also offers its archive on CD for a minor consideration.

Shareware.com

http://www.
shareware.com

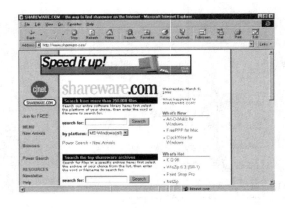

An American site
which delivers the
goods in its own
unique way.
Shareware.com has
a plethora of
archives dating
back quite some
time which allows the visitor to trace those hard to find
items that the "experts" have been using for ages. Its
unfriendly user interface can make it a little daunting for
the Internet beginner.

Download.com

http://www.
download.com

Yet another US site
which touts all the
latest shareware
and freeware
releases. Big, bold
graphics and use of
solid colours make
this a very
impressive site to look at – and it's backed up with top
quality content, making it ideal when searching for the Net
equivalent of fluffy dice and go-faster stripes for your PC.

Educational Resources

In spite of what you may have heard there are, in fact, many useful educational resources on the Internet. Here are some of the more valuable ones:

BBC Education

http://www.bbc.co.uk/education/

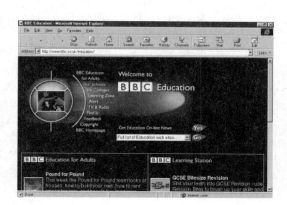

The best of the nation's broadcasting company is brought together here in one place.

For those who thought the BBC had abandoned informative programming in favour of mindless gameshows, think again!

National Geographic

http://www.national geographic.com/kids/

An excellent source of information relating to the natural world.

From pen pal link-ups to fascinating facts for the day, there's something here to keep everyone interested, informed and entertained.

Find a huge list of educational websites chosen by teachers at http://www. spartacus.schoolnet. co.uk/index.html

Encarta Online

http://encarta.msn.com/ EncartaHome.asp

Microsoft's huge electronic encyclopaedia is now available in a cut-down version on-line. With information covering more subjects than you can shake a stick at it's bound to come in handy at homework time.

Biography.com

http://www. biography.com

If they're hot, they're in. With the lowdown on more than 20,000 people throughout human history, biography.com provides all of the information you could ever want. From dictators to world leaders and rock stars, this easy to use, fully searchable database is packed to the hilt with useful stuff.

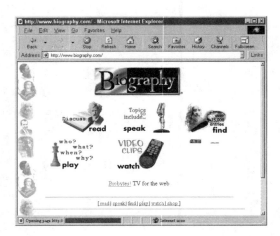

News Sites

HANDY TIP

Get the latest up-to-the-minute news from the company that provides for the dailies at http://www.pa.press.net

As the popularity of the Internet has captured the imagination of the UK public, so those in charge of the traditional media have sought to take their content and make it available on-line.

From TV listings magazines to daily newspapers and satellite news stations – they're all here.

The Times

http://www.the-times.co.uk

Probably the best known of Britain's broadsheet dailies, The Times has a strong on-line presence, releasing a portion of daily content relating to the daily news and sport. There's even a handy searchable archive which indexes articles from previous editions.

The Daily Star

http://www.megastar.co.uk

One of the most popular tabloids in the country runs this very in-yer-face site, which contains a handful of daily news stories but prefers to concentrate its efforts on entertainment rather than hard fact. Fun and frivolous, it captures the flavour of the paper and its tongue in cheek attitude.

The BBC

http://news.bbc.co.uk

Home and International news rub shoulders on the home site for the country's national broadcast TV station. Well designed and well executed, it makes for pleasant browsing.

Sky TV

http://www.sky.co.uk

Satellite giants BSkyB provide a wealth of information from their UK-based home site, ranging from news and weather reports to program schedules and features on up-coming goodies. It's cheaper than buying a programme listings guide and a good deal more pleasing to the eye!

Fun Sites

Ask any Net user what they're looking for from the Internet and they'll probably tell you "fun stuff".

There are hundreds and hundreds of sites dedicated to the pursuit of entertainment. Here are some of the better ones.

Shockrave

http://www.
shockrave.com

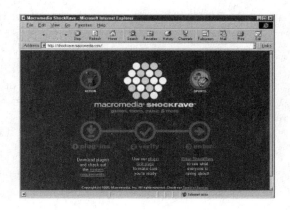

Part of the site run by multimedia experts Macromedia, Shockrave contains all manner of games and amusements created using their Shockwave browser plug-in (see chapter 3 for more on plug-ins).

From puzzles to arcade games, there's a little of something for everyone here.

Dilbert

http://www.
dilbert.com

No honest-to-God Net geek should be without this totally excellent URL.

The story of an office worker trapped in a sea of paperwork, this daily strip by US cartoonist Scott Adams is bound to strike a chord with office workers everywhere.

Toonograms

http://www.
toonogram.com

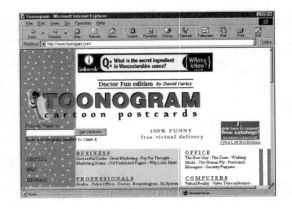

Everyone loves to receive a greetings card from a friend, and when it's a silly one it makes it all the better. Toonograms are free to send and free to receive, covering a wide variety of subjects from "Get Well" to "Bad Day at the Office".

Uproar

http://
www.uproar.com

If it's fun and entertainment you want then look no further than this excellent site.

Uproar has a little of everything: from on-line games to word puzzles, and a links section that ranges from dialect generators which translate your speech into Swedish Chef-style text to a superb avi of an exploding whale (it has to be seen to be believed...).

Web Resources

There comes a time when even the most technophobic of Internet users decides it's time to delve deeper into the wonderful (if slightly complicated) world of the Net.

Here are a few of the more accessible resource centres of the web.

W3C

http://www.w3.org

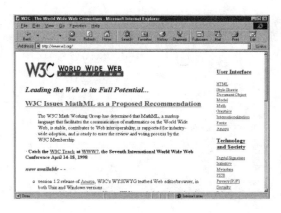

The W3C (World Wide Web Consortium) is the organisation which sets the standards the web runs upon.

An interesting (if techie) site if you're interested in the way the Web is woven.

A Brief History of the Net

http://
jrowse.mtx.net/net/
hype.html

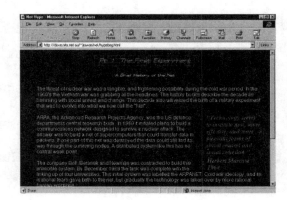

And in the beginning all was dark. Then the US military became terrified of Russian nuclear attack and thus the net was born (or something like that).

Check out this informative site for the truth about the roots of the Internet we know today.

NetHistory

http://www.geocities.
com/SiliconValley/
2260/

An extended look
at the early years
of BITNET and the
Internet, which
features archives
of original digital
documents and
articles written by those who helped to shape the virtual
communications world which is the modern Internet.

Internet History

http://www.
internetvalley.com/
intval.html

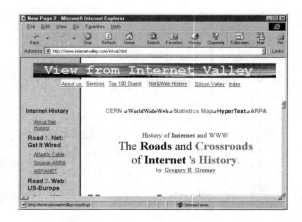

If it's Internet
history you're
looking for, look
no further than
this very excellent
site. The
information here
splits the net into geographical areas, starting with the US
and including Europe and the Far East, and provides an in-
depth look at the growth of net use in addition to facts and
figures in graphical format.

A must see for potential net historians.

Graphics

Everyone likes graphics, whether they're for use as webpage images or as wallpaper for the Windows desktop.

Try this small collection of top sites to get you started.

Fxtra

http://www.fxtra.com/hotstuff.htm

 If this talk of pretty pictures has inspired you, why not nip over to http:// digitalworkshop.co. uk/ and download Paintshop Pro, the Internet's favourite shareware art package.

Some wonderful graphic images for the taking here, courtesy of the people at fxtra. In addition there are a handful of digital tunes and animated GIFs which would sit lightly on anyone's PC.

Free Graphics Store

http:// ausmall.com.au/ freegraf/index.htm

Updated bi-weekly, this site contains dozens of image sets for every occasion. So if you need a dainty little something to spruce up a newsletter, or you're looking for an illuminated letter to liven your own webpages, stop by here and have a browse around.

Windy's Fashionable Designs

http://
www.windyweb.
com/design

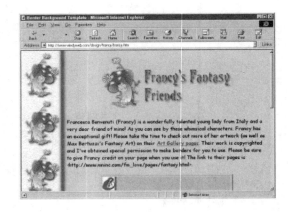

A beautifully designed site, featuring some excellent work from professional artists. The folk at Windy's have persuaded a number of their chums to part with the copyright on their images for the edification of the browsing public – what nice people they are!

Computer Graphics

http://mambo.ucsc.
edu/psl/cg.html

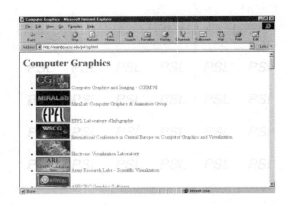

Containing just about every graphics-related link you could ever want, this site is not particularly pretty in its presentation, but then, presentation isn't everything.

From NASA through to commercial offerings and personal homepages – it's all here. Go ahead, take a peek!

Sounds

Computer graphics are great but there are times when a wee tune or two can really lift the spirits. Try some of the links below and see what fun can be had with sound.

HANDY TIP

Why not record your own soundfiles. Visit http://www. goldwave.com for a quality shareware sound package.

The Movie WAVs page

http://

www.moviewavs.com

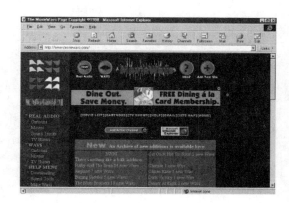

One of the more common formats used for sending sound over the Internet is the Wav, or wave. This excellent site contains dozens of them, and every one is a tasteful clip from the movie world.

Cartoon Sounds

http://

www.cartoonsounds.com

Fans of the animated arts will find the perfect audio compliment to their visuals here. The Simpsons, Beavis and Butthead and the smash hit South Park all have a home here.

WAV files

http://www.fastnet.
ndirect.co.uk/
sounds.htm

Short, sharp and to
the point. The
sound samples on
this regularly
updated website
can serve equally
well as spot effects

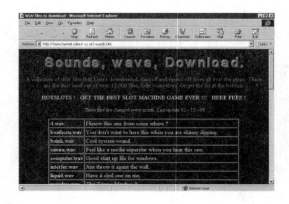

on homepages or as alert sounds for a PC or a Macintosh.
Excellent stuff.

WAV Central

http://www.
wavcentral.com/

A very professional
American site
which contains
some highly
polished sound
editing samples.

You may not
understand the
comedic content of all the clips but you have to admire the
technical skill behind it all.

Animations

Just the thing to liven up any webpage, there are plenty of places across the Net to find a wealth of resources dedicated to the creation of animated graphics.

Rose's Animated GIFs

http://www. wanderers2.com/ rose/animate1.html

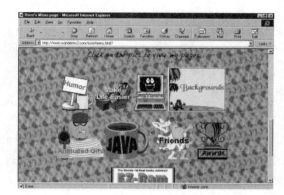

A great place to start that's in-yer-face and very useful indeed. All of the graphics on this site are free to download and use however and wherever you wish.

Andy's Art Attack

http://www. andyart.com

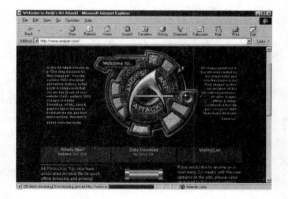

One of the most beautifully crafted sites on the web, Andy's Art Attack is a classic example of how to do web design properly.

Oh, and there are loads and loads of great free animated images mixed in with graphic creation tips and much, much more.

Making Animated GIFs

http://member.aol.com/royalef/gifmake.htm

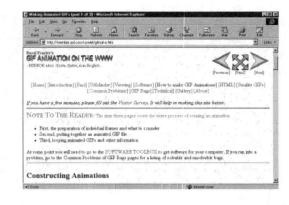

If you've followed any of the links on the previous page you may be wondering how these talented people created such fine works of moving art. Well, follow the instructions on this site and have a go yourself – you'll be amazed at how simple it really is!

First Internet Animation Festival

http://losangeles.digitalcity.com/animation/gifgalm.html

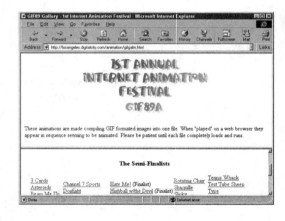

If you want to see the best the Net can offer in terms of its animated content, then spend a happy half hour browsing through this lot.

The entries for the First Internet Animation Festival were of a high standard indeed and the eventual winner – an animated GIF of a runaway mining car – was surely worthy of first prize. It's enough to make the less artistic among us green with envy!

Buying On-line

On-line shopping, or e-commerce as it's known, is set to be the Net's 'next big thing'.

![HANDY TIP hand icon] **The UK shopguide contains all manner of useful information on how to buy goods on-line. Visit http://www.shopguide.co.uk./about.html**

The advantages of buying over the Internet are great, offering shoppers the chance to part with their hard-earned cash without ever having to leave the comfort of their homes.

Here's a handful of ways to lighten your wallet...

BarclaySquare

http://www.barclaysquare.co.uk

A huge e-commerce shopping site created by the leading British bank, BarclaySquare has attracted a lot of interest from major High Street names. Well worth a look.

CDNow

http://www.cdnow.com

If you're looking to purchase some top tunes over the net, look no further than CDNow. One of the oldest of the Net's on-line music shopping centres, it displays a variety of features designed to ease the way you buy.

Freemans

http://www.
freemans.co.uk

Home site for the
popular mail order
catalogue people,
and a great example
of how to create a
good looking site
backed by quality
products.

 **For a more
compre-
hensive
coverage**
**of useful sites get
Internet Directory
UK in easy steps, in
this same series.**

Amazon

http://www.
amazon.com

There's no such
thing as too much
knowledge, and this
rather natty little
site is stuffed with
it. Browse through
millions of books,
CDs, DVDs and

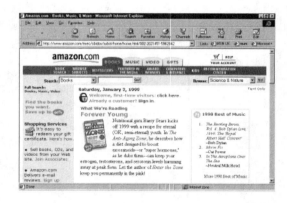

other gifts before paying for your selections on-line. The
perfect way to take the stress out of shopping!

Other Things To Do

As the Internet 'grows up' ingenious developers are finding ever new ways to harness its communications and entertainment potential.

In this chapter we'll take a look at some of the more unusual and exciting ways to use the Net to your own advantage.

Covers

Chapter Eleven

Net Telephony

In chapter nine we looked at the wonderful world of IRC, which allows its users to communicate wherever they may be in the world through a real-time text chat client.

However, while text is great, there's nothing quite like hearing or even seeing (see later in this chapter) the person you're chatting with.

 If your PC didn't come equipped with a microphone you can use any standard mic which has a suitable jack fitting.

In order to ease this process there are several firms who produce net telephony software.

All that's required is your Net connection (obviously), a soundcard (most PCs come with them fitted as standard) and a microphone.

If you have the basics, just download and install the software and arrange to be on-line at the same time as the person you want to chat with.

Apart from being easy to install and use, the major advantage of using such a system is cost. If you regularly converse with family or friends abroad you'll know how costly it can be. Using net telephony software all you pay is the cost of connecting to your Internet Access Provider, which in the majority of cases is simply a local rate call through British Telecom.

To use your Internet connection to make a phone call, try the trial version of Internet phone from:

http://www.vocaltec.com/iphone.htm

On-line Games

Everyone loves games – whether it's a battle of wits over the chessboard or the chance to blast the forces of darkness all the way down to Hell in Doom. The Internet can make these experiences all the better.

Until fairly recently, computer gaming was a solitary affair, pitting a single user against his or her own PC, unless you happened to be attached to an office network (and there are very few bosses who like to see company equipment being used for gaming purposes...).

It is very easy to get sucked into the world of on-line gaming and rack up a huge phone bill without realising. If you are running to a phone budget (or have unsympathetic parents) be warned!

Increasingly these days, PC software houses are building Internet options into their products which opens up whole new vistas for the electronic gaming fan.

The advantage of Internet play is that it's now possible to pit your skills against opponents from around the world, using the Net as the transport tool to keep your machine and that of your erstwhile opponent fully aware of the current situation.

Even better, some of the more advanced titles allow multiple players to compete in the same gaming arena, and even to form coherent 'sides' which face off against one another in on-going tournament competitions.

Possibly the best examples of such titles are the mighty Quake II and LucasArts Star Wars classic X-Wing vs TIE Fighter.

Quake II has been hailed as one of the greatest computer games of all time. It puts the player in an imaginary underground cave system populated by all manner of grotesque creatures. In the single player game the objective is a simple one – to explore the various levels of the dungeon annihilating anything which gets in the way.

The real power of the game comes from the multi-player, or deathmatch, mode which has become so popular with gamers the world over that it has spawned global leagues, creating media celebrities from its better players and even cash prize competitions worth thousands of dollars/pounds.

X-Wing vs TIE Fighter caused a similar surge of interest, putting prospective spacecraft pilots up against one another in the continuing struggle of good against evil.

It's not all 25th Century stuff however and it's perfectly possible to indulge in anything from a soothing game of Mah Jong to a battle of wits over Risk if you know where to look.

One of the hottest sites in the UK relates to British Telecom's Wireplay service, a games-only online facility which is dedicated to giving the home player the very best in electronic entertainment.

Their site at http://www.wireplay.co.uk contains full details on what's hot and what's not, special offers on a variety of products and much more.

Video Conferencing

Earlier this chapter we took a look into the world of Net telephony and examined how it is possible to chat with people around the globe over an Internet connection.

Taking a step up from that technology is the relatively new world of video conferencing and chat which, perhaps unsurprisingly, allows you to see and hear the person with whom you are conversing.

So far so good, but unlike its poor relation, video conferencing can be an expensive hobby.

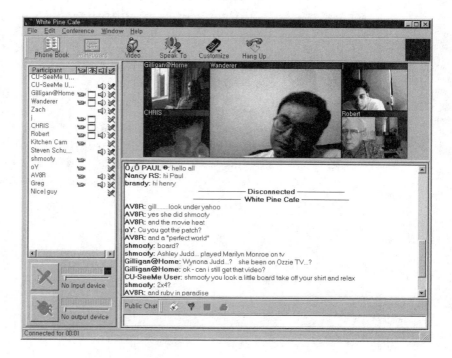

The first thing you'll need is a special digital camera in order to take pictures of yourself which will be sent to the other party. Such cameras start at around £70 for a simple black and white model up to several hundred pounds for the colour versions.

The cost of the camera is not the only expense, and it should be borne in mind that the specialist software required to run the camera in conjunction with the Net connection (for instance the excellent CU-SeeMe from White Pine – http://www.wpine.com) may also cost you a pretty penny.

Currently, video conferencing is a classic example of how the complexity of modern software can outstrip the potential of the Internet. TV quality pictures are out of the question at the moment as a result of the restrictions placed on data traffic by the general speed of the Internet. But if you can cope with the sound being a little stilted from time to time, and the occasional glitch on the picture (which is usually pretty small it has to be said), then this form of communication is ideal.

So, if you can bear the cost of the component parts and cope with the odd technical glitch, video conferencing can be great fun, and like using telephony software it can be a very cheap way to keep in touch – don't forget, the only call charges you'll pay are local charges to your ISP; after that all of your communications are conducted over the Internet.

Sending an E-fax

For many people, fax machines are still something that you keep in the office and don't let into the home.

However, for those who have thought from time to time how handy it would be to send a quick fax off to confirm a purchase order or give someone directions to their home, help is at hand.

The incredibly thoughtful people at UK ISP Demon Internet have teamed up with The Phone Company to provide a global e-mail to fax service.

HANDY TIP

An increasing number of desktop modems are already equipped to send and receive faxes. It is the work of only a few moments to set yours up and install the software necessary to turn your home computer into a part-time fax machine.

All that's required is to fill in an on-line form for plain text, or download a special client program if you see the need to send images, diagrams and the like, then hit the Send button.

Your fax message is bundled up in e-mail form and passed through some special software which works out where the nearest e-mail centre to the intended destination is. The mail is sent off in a flash and decoded at the remote site before being sent to the recipient's fax machine.

As with many things Net-related, this procedure is a relatively inexpensive one if you intend to send data out of the country as it only costs the price of a local phone call to get your message away.

For more information on the service visit:

http://www.demon.net/services/fax

E-mail to Snail Mail

As soon as someone comes along with a great idea to do one thing (for instance sending e-mail to fax messages) you can bet that pretty soon someone else will come along and top it – it's the way of the Net.

In this case the new kids on the block are partners MSN, the Microsoft Network, and the Royal Mail. They have hit upon the idea of providing a service in which electronic documents can be converted into paper ones for standard mail delivery.

At first glance this may seem rather pointless: the purpose of e-mail is to reduce the amount of paper floating around the office, not increase it. But take a moment to think about it and the possibilities become obvious.

Electronic documents (even in these enlightened times) are still not convenient for every occasion – it's sometimes better that a business proposal or personal greeting, for example, be sent by traditional means. Bear in mind also that not everyone has access to e-mail and that ordinary or snail mail (as it's known to many Net users) is often the only way to get the message through.

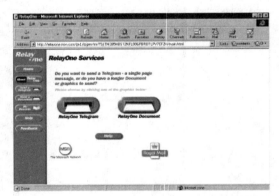

Either way, the Relay One service does have its uses. All it takes is a few mouse clicks and the entry of some details and the Royal mail will guarantee next day delivery of your files within the UK (although documents heading out of the country will take a while longer).

For more information visit:

http://www.relayone.msn.com

Telnet, MUDs and MOOs

A long time before the World Wide Web began to weave its spell over the Internet, there were a number of ways in which users could access files and information.

Many of these methods – which had bizarre names like Jughead and Veronica – have fallen by the wayside but some still remain. One of the most popular is Telnet.

Telnet allows the user to log on to a remote Net-connected computer and allows the user's own machine to act as a dumb terminal. In this way it can be used to issue commands to the remote machine.

HANDY TIP For a full list of MUDs visit http://www. mudconnector.com

For the most part this is redundant now, as all of the information that was once available via Telnet is freely accessible through the Web. Nevertheless, one area in which Telnet does still excel is in its ability to allow those interested to connect to MUDs and MOOs.

MUDs (or Multi-User Dungeons) are multi-player games, usually text only, which resemble the computer adventure games of old. Hundreds of individuals can connect up simultaneously and either chat with one another or go off on pre-set tasks set in a multitude of worlds.

All of the commands are entered through the keyboard, giving the whole thing an appearance similar to that of IRC (see chapter 9 for more details). However, the MUD differs in that it's a pre-created and strictly controlled world which is administered by a set of super-users who can dictate who will take part in the game and how the game world looks. MOOs, or Multi-User Dungeon-Object-Orientated, are simply a variation on this theme: the difference lies in the way the software behind the virtual world can be configured by those in charge.

The great thing about such games is the scope and variety of the projects. Some of them have been operating for years without a break and have evolved from simple, small virtual worlds into huge, sprawling communities which users log into to chat with friends or to immerse themselves in the subject matter of the 'world'.

From the hack-and-slash brutality of Dungeons and Dragons, through gangster worlds of the 1920s and on to the bleak Sci-Fi future created by William Gibson, there is something here for everyone. Best of all, it's totally free!

For the truly ambitious it is even possible to set up your own virtual world using free software packages (which are available from a number of sources across the Internet) and a little time and patience. Be warned however that it is not an easy task to accomplish, and you should have a great deal of confidence in your abilities before you attempt it.

If you don't fancy using Telnet to access the MUDs and MOOs you're not going to lose out. A number of the newer and more forward thinking sites are turning towards Java-based solutions which run from within a web browser. This is excellent news for the continued popularity and success of these virtual universes. If you fancy jumping straight in at the deep end, try a Cyberpunk-based world in Swansea by starting your Telnet client, entering rsushi.swansea.ac.uk as the address and giving 5500 as the port number.

Creating Your Own Web Pages

There are tens of thousands of web pages sitting out there on the World Wide Web, just waiting to be discovered. In this chapter we'll take a look at how you can further swell that number by creating your own.

Chapter Twelve

Covers

Why Have One?

It's a silly question and it deserves a silly answer – why not?

Until the advent of the World Wide Web, having your material published was a tricky task to achieve. Unless you had the time to sit down and write a 400 page best-seller, or were a journalist of one kind or another, your chances of getting anything within sight of a printing press were limited in the extreme.

Happily, all that changed with the advent of the Internet and its rapid growth in popularity. Because it's an electronic medium there are no expensive printing costs to take into account. And with the cost of computing equipment falling almost weekly it has become a relatively simple matter for companies and organisations to provide space on their net-connected computers for individuals and firms to sell both themselves and their wares to anyone who wants them.

It's not all about consumerism of course. The vast majority of the Web's tens of thousands of pages are written and maintained by private individuals who want to tell the world a little about themselves and their lives.

Some of these sites have become massively popular in their own right and developed into businesses – Yahoo!, one of the world's biggest search engines, started life as a single page of links to its creator's favourite web sites.

Not all of the pages out there are as useful as Yahoo! but the range of quality and content held on the Web make for varied viewing experiences.

Whatever the rights and wrongs of good or bad design and content provision, the great thing about the Web is that anyone can have their 15 minutes of fame through their own web creations.

Choosing Material

It's all too easy to go rushing into the creation of your first publishing opus and produce a horrific mess.

Careful forethought is required!

Many, many people are so eager to put anything up in front of the world that they rush a couple of pages of material out without any thought whatsoever. They then draw sack-loads of critical e-mail from site visitors who've had a quick look and then disappeared, never to return.

The first thing any self-respecting e-author should think about is what the content of the new site will be.

Broadly speaking there are only a small number of different types of web site:

* Personal sites about the author

* Sites relating to a business

* Fan sites, dedicated to football clubs, rock bands, etc.

* Electronic publications/guides and help sites

After deciding what kind of site you would like to produce you should consider what your site can contribute. In the case of the personal site this question is immaterial. But if you were producing a site relating to your favourite band or soccer club do you have anything new and interesting to contribute, or do you intend to cull your content from existing sites on the Net?

If you have a fresh, new view on things – congratulations! Your site is already one step up the ladder to success and popularity.

If you intend to take material from other sites, ask yourself what the point is, and bear in mind that popular subjects like soccer and movies like Star Trek (perennial Net favourites) are subject to stringent copyright laws. If you take copyright material from an official site, be warned: some organisations WILL take legal action.

Web Space

With your ideas in place it's time to put them into action, and the first step in the implementation is to find somewhere to put (or host) them.

Today the vast majority of UK-based ISPs provide their subscribers with free web space to some extent at least. Most of these providers will allow you between five and ten megabytes of storage for your material, and some allow more – Somerset-based UKOnline (http://www.ukonline.co.uk) offer an unlimited amount of space.

Knowing your limits here is very important. Exceeding the storage space may mean parts of your site never see the light of day and some providers may charge if you go over by a significant amount. Be sure to check what the limits are and to keep a watchful eye on how much material you're putting together.

If you happen to be a subscriber to one of the services which doesn't give you free space – fear not! There are several organisations around which will give you space for free, even if you're not a subscriber.

US-based Geocities (http://www.geocities.com) has thousands of users, none of whom pay for the space they use. It's fair to say that the amount of space provided is quite a lot smaller than with some firms, but hey, it's free!

Whoever you go to for space, be sure to read their acceptable use policy before planning your site. Some organisations place very rigid rules and regulations on what is and is not acceptable. This rule points quite obviously at 'adult' material, but quite a few providers forbid anyone posting what they deem to be commercial sites, as these are usually paid for, and in some cases actually help finance the provision of the free personal web space.

Creating Your Pages

With a masterplan in place and storage space organised it's time to start building your masterpiece.

Unfortunately, this is probably the trickiest stage in the entire process.

As the more inquisitive among you will already have discovered, it is necessary to learn to use a special Web programming language called HTML (HyperText Markup Language) to turn ordinary and boring text into exciting, colourful web pages.

 For more information on HTML, try the HTML book in this same series.

HTML comprises dozens of special commands which, when interpreted by the browser, allow a range of basic formatting commands to be executed. These vary from creating special item lists through to changing font colour and size.

Over the years the specification from the HTML language has been continually tweaked and updated in order to keep up with the times. Perhaps the biggest change since its inception occurred around the middle of 1997 with the introduction of Dynamic HTML.

Unlike the ordinary, static HTML in which it's impossible to move any of the on-screen elements once they've been placed, Dynamic HTML (DHTML) allows the page creator to build interactivity in. This is made possible by an incredible degree of control over sound and graphical elements as well as the facility to change text 'on the fly'.

The downside to using a technology such as DHTML is that to make it work takes a degree of technical skill slightly above that of the beginner.

To get the best from the many faces of Dynamic HTML requires an understanding of a scripting language such as JavaScript or Visual Basic Script.

Such scripting languages are more like established full-blown computer programming languages than the basic page layout instructions of standard HTML.

HTML Avoided

Having established that HTML is the only way to place your pearls of wisdom onto the World Wide Web, and that HTML can be a little tricky to learn, the obvious question is 'How can we avoid it altogether?'

Fortunately for the technically challenged, and those who don't have the time to sit down and learn a whole new language, there are a number of solutions to the problem.

Today there are a growing number of WYSIWYG (What You See Is What You Get) page creation packages on the market and also a number of other programs which are capable of outputting HTML code.

The dedicated packages include Microsoft's excellent FrontPage program and Macromedia's Dynamic HTML compatible Dreamweaver software. Both are incredibly easy to use and come with a variety of extras, including graphics creation programs. FrontPage even includes a special program to help administer, publish and maintain your web creations.

HANDY TIP

Computer Step also publish, FrontPage in easy steps.

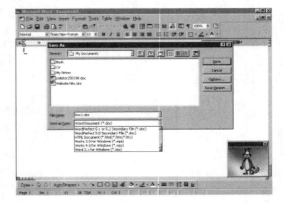

For those who wish to experiment without paying money for specialist tools, check out the Save As options built into your word processor. Microsoft's latest Word package (part of the Office suite) has a special option built-in which allows your word processor documents to be exported in a web compatible format – it doesn't come any easier than that!

Testing Your Pages

Almost as important as creating the pages in the first place is testing them before they 'go live'.

It is very easy just to throw some HTML together, add a few links to your favourite sites and then post the whole package in the direction of a server without making sure everything is intact.

At the simplest level you should always check the 'in-site' links which connect all of your own pages together. It's not a difficult task (unless you have an unusually large Web site) and you'd be surprised at how many errors you'll pick up: from images which display incorrectly or not at all to spelling errors in the text (many HTML authoring tools come complete with a spell-checker and it seems a shame not to use it if it's free!).

This first level checking can be done off-line, which avoids dial-up charges and allows you to take a good, long look at your creation.

Perhaps slightly more difficult is checking up on the validity of external or 'off-site' links. We all have our favourite sites on the Net and it's often nice to be able to present them to site visitors or to provide links which are associated with the subject matter you have selected for your publishing opus.

The problem comes when site URLs are typed incorrectly, or are no longer around – the nature of the Web is such that some sites will surface for a few weeks or months and then disappear for ever with no rhyme or reason.

To avoid the embarrassment of broken and missing links make sure you check them all before uploading your site.

There's nothing worse than visiting a beautifully designed and content-rich site only to find it's littered with images which won't load and links that don't lead anywhere.

Publishing Your Work

OK, so the site has been designed, the pages put together and (hopefully) the links all checked and found to be working.

The next step is to put your site in the path of the viewing public.

Try to ensure the first page of your site is called 'index. htm' or 'index.html' as this will ensure the page is displayed 'automatically' whenever someone types in the URL of your site. Some sites prefer you to use content.html so check with your provider.

Perhaps surprisingly, this is the easiest step of the entire creation process and involves gratuitous use of a good FTP client (see chapter 6 for more information on what FTP is and how it works).

Most important in this procedure is that you find out the details required to set up an FTP connection with your web server of choice. Many providers will issue you with a special address to which you should upload the files and a username and password to match.

If you're storing information in space provided by your ISP you may find you will use your standard dial-up username and password for this purpose, although some firms will issue special, separate ones. It's a certainty that if your web space is held by someone other than your ISP, you will definitely have new log-in details.

Once you're connected it's simply a matter of selecting the files to publish and hitting the Upload button. When this operation is complete, wait a few seconds and type in the Web address for your page – the content should appear before your eyes!

For the cash-rich it's possible to 'buy' your own address which you can then 'point' to your web space, so if you fancy having www.thisismywebsite.co.uk you can do so!

For more information on web domain name registration visit **Corpex** at http://www.corpex.co.uk. Be warned, it can cost anything from £60 and upwards to register the name for two years so it's not the world's cheapest form of vanity publishing, but if image is important it is better to have to spend a few pounds than point people to www.someserver.co.uk/public/~users/myspace/!

Updating Pages

Someone once said of the newspaper industry that the news of today is the fish and chip paper of tomorrow. The same can (virtually) be said of the Web.

Information which is new to the world at the moment can quickly become outdated, second even to pages which are broken. The biggest turn off for web viewers is old content.

Of course, the concept of 'fresh' content may not apply to all sites (after all information on the American Civil War isn't going to change very often ...).

That said, it's always good to have a re-think now and again and change the look and feel of your site, even if you don't do much with the actual content.

The thing to bear in mind is that there are tens of thousands of other sites on the Web at large and if there is any degree of competitive spirit about you, you'll want yours to be the best and the most visited.

Obviously, sites which change regularly, like those to football clubs for example, are going to need at least a weekly update throughout the playing season. Such updates can be extremely time consuming. Less demanding sites can be altered in a number of subtle ways to make it seem as though alterations have been carried out.

The easiest way to achieve such an effect is to change a colour scheme or alter a few graphics here and there – you would be amazed at the difference such a cosmetic change can make.

It's always nice, however, to look at your site every couple of months and decide if a complete overhaul is required. A really good spring clean every now and again works wonders for a site that's looking a little dusty.

Advanced Options

As a general guideline, never be afraid to experiment with your web designs and add a few of the latest goodies that can be discovered from around the Net.

Basic HTML-based pages are all well-and-good but a Java applet here and there or a spot of Dynamic HTML code can really supply a bit of 'vavoom' to your work.

HANDY TIP

Use the Web Page Design in easy steps book in this same series.

Because of the decidedly friendly nature of the Internet there are plenty of people who offer you such goodies to play with for free. You don't even need to know how they work as the programmers normally provide full instructions with the code segments. All you have to do is insert the code into your pages and off you jolly well go!

If you're wondering why anyone would want to put all that effort into creating a web masterpiece and then just give it away the answer is simple – they're just very nice people! Another answer is that there are firms who produce such programs for a living and who give them away to individuals for free, but often charge companies a licence fee to use the snippet on their commercial websites.

A great place to start in the hunt for some groovy gadgets is the aptly named Developer.com (http://www. developer.com) which is a fully searchable repository of tools ranging from page counters, which allow you to track

the number of visitors to your site, through to entire arcade games written in Java which will happily sit inside your web pages.

Glossary

The Internet overflows with technical terms and TLAs (three letter acronyms, for the uninitiated).

In this chapter we present a list of the more popular phrases. Whilst many have been used in this book, others haven't but may be useful at some time in the future.

Glossary

ActiveX
A Microsoft technology that facilitates information sharing among applications. It is primarily used for developing interactive applications and Web content.

Applet
A computer program written in Java™. Applets are similar to applications, but they don't run as stand-alones. Instead, applets conform to a set of conventions that let them run within a Java-compatible browser.

ARPAnet
The acronym for *Advanced Research Project Agency*, the U.S. Department of Defence agency that funded the development of the first computers that linked networks across great distances. The ARPAnet was the forerunner of the Internet.

Attachment
A file delivered as part of an e-mail message.

Backbone
The central network infrastructure of the Internet. It enables information to be transmitted from one Internet access provider to another.

Bandwidth
The amount of data that can be sent through a connection before the carrier becomes full, usually measured in bits per second (bps). A fast modem is capable of moving 30 thousand bits per second.

Baud
(Pronounced bawd) The speed at which a modem or other device is capable of transmitting data, technically measured in number of events, or signal changes, per second. (Baud rate is commonly, but incorrectly, assumed to mean the number of bits per second, which is not the same measurement.)

...cont'd

HANDY TIP To learn more about the way your browser works, visit http://browserwatch. internet.com

Bookmark

Many browsers allow users to set electronic bookmarks to ease the process of surfing the web. The bookmark is merely a link to a favourite web site which is held in a special file on your hard disk and can be called up with the click of a button, rather than leaving the user to remember long and complicated URLs to sites.

Browser

A software program used to view World Wide Web content and also to retrieve and display copies of files in an easy-to-read format. Modern browsers can draw upon associated programs to play audio and video files.

HANDY TIP The birthplace of the World Wide Web has a home on the Internet – http:// www.cern.ch/

CERN

Conseil Européenne pour la Recherche Nucléaire, the European Laboratory for Particle Physics in Geneva, Switzerland, where in the 1980s a team of pioneering engineers led by Tim Berners-Lee developed the World Wide Web technology.

CGI

Short for *Common Gateway Interface*, software that allows communication between a web server and programs operating outside the server – for example, code that processes interactive forms or which searches databases on the server for information requested by a user.

Clients

Software programs that provide access to network resources by working with the information on a *server*.

Cookie

A file stored on your hard disk and used to identify your computer or your preferences to a remote computer. Cookies are frequently used to identify visitors to web sites.

Content

The collective name for the text, pictures, sound, data, or other information presented by a web site.

Cyber-

Prefix for anything to do with computers or the Internet (eg, put a computer in the corner and your favourite café becomes a cybercafé).

Cyberspace

William Gibson coined the phrase Cyberspace in his novel 'Neuromancer.' It is widely available from a variety of on-line bookstores, including Waterstones (http://waterstones.co.uk).

The virtual universe of information transmitted by computers, programs, audio and video media, telephone and television, wire, and satellite. The phrase was coined by sci-fi writer William Gibson, who defined it as: "A graphical representation of data abstracted from the banks of every computer in the human system."

Domain Name

The Internet name of a computer or group of computers. The domain name usually defines the name of an organisation, its geographical position and the type of site (commercial, educational, military, etc). In the example fictitious.uk.com the domain describes the company (fictitious), the location (UK) and its type (COMmercial).

Downloading

The process of requesting and transferring a file from a remote computer to a local computer and saving the file on the local computer, usually via a modem or network.

E-mail

A means of sending typed messages from one computer to another over the Internet or a network.

FAQs

Short for *Frequently Asked Questions*, a list of questions and answers in response to queries users have relating to a specific topic.

Firewall

Software intended to prevent unauthorized access to a computer network.

Flame

An e-mail or newsgroup posting composed with the intention of causing offence or outrage.

...cont'd

 FTP and other shareware packages can be downloaded from http://tucows. cableinet.co.uk

Freeware
Copyrighted software available at no charge from the software's author and often available over the Internet.

FTP
Short for *File Transfer Protocol*, an Internet protocol that allows users to transfer files to and from other computers.

GIF (or .gif)
Stands for *Graphics Interchange Format*, a type of graphic file format suitable for use in World Wide Web documents.

Gigabyte
A measurement of electronic file size equalling roughly one billion bytes.

Home Page
The main page of a Web site. Home pages generally contain text and links to locations within the site, or to external sites.

HTML
Short for *Hypertext Markup Language*, HTML is the language used to create and layout documents for the World Wide Web.

HTTP
Short for *Hypertext Transfer Protocol*, the protocol which is the basis of World Wide Web technology. HTTP is the set of rules governing the software that transports HTML documents along the Internet.

Hyperlink
A reference or link which, when clicked, will automatically transfer an Internet user to another page or site on the Internet. (Hyperlinks may also be used to link to specific points on the page which contain the link itself.)

Hypertext

Electronic text in a format that provides instant access, via *links*, to other hypertext within a document or in another document.

Internet

In its most general sense, an internet is a large computer network made up of a number of smaller networks. When capitalized, it refers to the physical network that makes up the Web and makes global e-mail possible.

Intranet

A private network within an organization. Intranets frequently use Internet protocols to deliver content. Often protected from the Internet by firewalls.

IP Address

The *Internet Protocol* address of a computer connected to the Internet, usually represented in dot/decimal notation, as in *128.121.4.5*

ISDN

Short for *Integrated Services Digital Network,* a network that acts as a digital-connection service for telephones and other communication devices. An ISDN connection can provide relatively high-speed access (up to 128,000 bits per second) to the Internet.

Java is a relatively new programming language on the Net. Its makers, Sun Microsystems, have a site dedicated to it at http://www.sun.com/java/index.html

ISP

Short for *Internet Service Provider*, a service that provides organisations and home users with access, via the ISP's servers, to the Internet.

Java

An object-oriented programming language developed by Sun Microsystems. It is used to create applets or programs which can be attached to Web documents. An applet can be included in an HTML page, much as an image can be included. When you use a Java-capable browser to view a page containing a Java applet, the applet's code is transferred to your system and executed by the browser.

 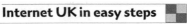

JPG or JPEG
Short for *Joint Photographic Experts Group*, a type of graphic file format suitable for use in web documents.

LAN
Acronym for *Local Area Network*, a network connecting two or more computers within a relatively small area, often the premises of an organisation, for the purpose of communicating and file-sharing.

Lurking
'Listening to' (reading) a newsgroup's discussion without participating in the on-going chats.

Megabyte
A measurement of electronic file size equalling one million bytes.

Modem
Stands for *Modulator/demodulator,* a hardware device that connects one computer to other computers, or to the Internet, over a standard telephone line. A modem can be either *internal* (built into a computer) or *external*. Modems are categorized by the speed at which they deliver data, measured in baud. Today's standard modems operate at 28,800 or 33,600 baud and even 56,000 baud.

Multimedia
Term for any content that combines text, sound, graphics, and/or video.

Net
An abbreviation for the Internet.

Netiquette
The combination of *Net* and *etiquette*, an unwritten code of rules for preserving civility on, and efficient use of, the Internet.

Newbie
Condescending term for an inexperienced user, or someone who is new to the Internet.

Newsgroups

Groups or forums on the Usenet in which users can share information, ideas, tips, and opinions on a particular subject. Newsgroups are organised by topics that number in the thousands.

Off-line

A phrase used to describe a computer which is not connected to the Internet.

On-line

A phrase used to describe a computer which is connected to the Internet.

Page

An individual frame of content on the World Wide Web, defined by a single HTML file and referenced by a single URL.

Platform

The hardware and system software that are the basic foundation of a computer system.

HANDY TIP

The Browser-watch site is a great place to find new plug-ins. Visit http:// browserwatch. internet.com

Plug-in

A software component or module that extends the capability of web browsers. Plug-ins enable the display of rich content such as audio, video, and animation.

PPP

Abbreviation for *Point-to-Point Protocol,* a configuration used to connect two computers with either a phone line or a network link that acts like a phone line.

Protocol

A system of rules or standards for communicating over a network, particularly the Internet. Computers and networks interact according to protocols that determine the behaviour each side expects from the other in the transfer of information.

Script or Scripting Language

A programming shortcut that gives non-technical users a way to create richer content on their computers and gives programmers a quick way to create simple applications.

Search Engine

A software application or service used to locate files on an intranet or the Web. Generally accessed with browsers, a few of the most common web search engines include Excite, Yahoo!, WebCrawler, Infoseek, and Lycos, but new search engines are added constantly.

Server

A computer, or its software, that 'serves' other computers on a network by administering files and network operations.

Shareware

Software that is available for a free try-out, but for which the author or developer requests payment if you decide to keep the software. Frequently, shareware is developed by small companies or individual programmers who set out to solve a specific computing problem or develop a novel application. In some cases, when you send payment, you will receive documentation along with the software.

Signature

An e-mail or Usenet feature that indicates who sent a message and/or where the message originated.

Site

A collection of related web pages, residing on the same server and interconnected by hotlinks.

SLIP

Serial Line Interface Protocol, this is a type of dial-up protocol used to connect a computer to the Internet.

SPAM
Electronic garbage and junk postings, often of a commercial nature, typically sent to many uninterested recipients.

Streamed Audio
Sound files captured in an audio file or transmitted over the Internet in real time. A plug-in to a web browser decompresses and plays the data as it is transferred to your computer over the Web. Streaming audio or video eliminates the delay that results when you download an entire file and then play it with a helper application.

String
A set of alpha-numeric characters used as input to calculations or searches.

Surf
Slang for 'to browse the Internet.' Can refer to browsing aimlessly, rather than seeking out specific content.

Tags
The formatting codes used to create HTML documents.

TCP/IP
Short for *Transmission Control Protocol* and *Internet Protocol*, the two protocols that govern the way computers and networks manage the flow of information over the Internet.

Telnet
A terminal emulation program used for logging on to other computers, especially large, mainframe computers such as those containing the on-line catalogues of libraries. When you use Telnet to log on to a library's computerised catalogue, you are gaining access to the files that constitute the library's records.

Threads
Used to organise Newsgroup (or Usenet) topics, a thread is like an online conversation made up of linked postings sent to a message poster or a conference.

Uploading

The process of transferring a file from a local computer to a remote computer via a modem or network.

URL

Short for *Uniform Resource Locator*, the address that specifies the electronic location of an Internet resource (file). A URL usually consists of four parts: protocol, server (or domain), path, and file name – although sometimes there will not be a path or file name.

Usenet

A system of electronic bulletin boards on which readers can share information, ideas, tips, and opinions. Nowadays usually referred to as *Newsgroups*.

Virtual Reality

Computer-generated 3-D space which simulates an organic physical environment.

Virus

HANDY TIP

A great starting place for protecting your PC against harmful viruses can be found at http:// www.drsolomon.com

With reference to computers, a malicious, human-created program that searches out other programs and 'infects' them by embedding a copy of itself. When an infected program runs, the virus is activated. A virus may passively reside for a while within a computer, unknown to the user, sometimes spreading to other locations, or it may run immediately. When it runs, it can have any number of effects, ranging from the appearance of annoying but harmless messages on the computer screen to destroying files on the computer's hard disk. Computer viruses are spread by the introduction of files into a computer from another computer, via disk or over a network (including the Internet). A wise computer user will make use of an up-to-date anti-virus program, available commercially by downloading from numerous Internet sites.

VRML

Short for *Virtual Reality Modelling Language*, a set of codes used for writing the files for three-dimensional, virtual reality programs.

W3 Consortium (W3C)

An industry consortium headed by the Laboratory for Computer Science at the Massachusetts Institute of Technology in Cambridge, Massachusetts (W3 refers to the World Wide Web). The consortium promotes standards and encourages inter-operability among World Wide Web products. Originally based at the European Laboratory for Particle Physics (CERN) in Geneva, Switzerland, where the World Wide Web technology was developed, the Consortium has had modest success in fostering co-operation on web technologies among a number of private corporations that are often reluctant to share their secrets.

Web (the)

Short for the World Wide Web.

Wizard

Computer-based help that guides you through the steps necessary to complete a task.

World Wide Web or WWW

A collection of multimedia content, connected by hyperlinks and providing an easy, graphical interface for navigating the Internet.

Index